Peter Ralston

To our readers

TO THE MARINER approaching Penobscot Bay at night from the south, the great lights of Monhegan and Matinicus Rock are this coast's first official messengers. They announce that shelter is at hand, but warn that attaining it will require caution and care. The flashes of their beacons on the distant horizon are confirmation, after a long night of waiting and watching, that the vessel's course has been true.

A lighthouse speaks of the relationship between people and the world around them, of the web of connections we humans have woven between ourselves and the sea upon which we depend. A lighthouse is a reminder, as it guides us to safety, that only by caring for others — for our community — can we survive.

This twelfth issue of *Island Journal* is fundamentally about communities, aggregations of people joined in common purpose. They live in places as different from one another as Bangor and Stonington, Vinalhaven and Campobello, Chebeague and Boston, Isle au Haut and the western coast of Ireland. Without exception their futures are problematic as they face the global problems and challenges of fisheries depletion, changing markets and ceaseless technological innovation.

These communities are not strictly human. The plants and animals that together make up an island's ecosystem are a community, as is the Penobscot River that daily injects millions of gallons of fresh water into its estuary and Penobscot Bay. So is the marine system that nurtures the great fisheries of the Gulf of Maine. Damage or deplete any of these natural communities, we have (again) been painfully reminded in recent months, and we run the real risk that they will not be there to sustain us in the future.

But relentlessly, the beam of a lighthouse pierces the gloom, reassuring the mariner that someone cares and that behind the flashing but momentary brightness, people are rewinding the weights that keep the lights revolving and the bells tolling, reminding us all that our planet is a community that thrives when each of us takes responsibility for others, every day we live.

— *the Editors*
Island Journal, 1995

ISLAND JOURNAL

The Annual Publication of the Island Institute
Volume Twelve

pg. 9

pg. 12

pg. 31

pg. 46

pg. 80

pg. 64

Departments

Cover photo by Peter Ralston

**ISLAND
INSTITUTE**
Publishers of Island Journal

Sustaining Islands And Their Communities

ISLAND JOURNAL

PUBLISHER
Philip W. Conkling

ART DIRECTOR
Peter Ralston

EXECUTIVE EDITOR
David D. Platt

ASSOCIATE EDITOR
Cynthia Bourgeault

COPY EDITOR
Anne C. R. Leslie

DESIGN & PRODUCTION
Michael Mahan Graphics
Bath, Maine

PRINTING
Penmor Lithographers
Lewiston, Maine

ISLAND INSTITUTE

PRESIDENT
Philip W. Conkling

EXECUTIVE VICE PRESIDENT
Peter Ralston

MANAGER, OPERATIONS AND FINANCE
Josée L. Shelley, CPA

FINANCIAL ASSISTANT
Michael P. Payne

COMMUNITY SERVICES DIRECTOR
Lisa Shields

ISLAND SCHOOLS DIRECTOR
James W. W. Wilmerding

SCIENCE AND STEWARDSHIP
Annette S. Naegel

PUBLICATIONS
David D. Platt, Ann Parrent, Sandra Smith

MARINE RESEARCH ASSOCIATES
Spencer Apollonio, Ted Ames

ASSOCIATE DEVELOPMENT DIRECTOR
Robin McIntosh

MEMBERSHIP DIRECTOR
Alan Conant

EXECUTIVE SECRETARY
Carol A. Smith

RECEPTIONIST
Jody A. Herbert

Peter Ralston (4)

RAVEN in Rockland harbor

EYE OF THE *RAVEN*
Journeys along the Archipelago

PHILIP W. CONKLING

ACH YEAR by early January when the sun etches a low arc on the gray rim of sky, you get a foretelling of winter's tales. The day after New Year's an intense but small northeast storm cell pinwheeled its way down the coast, scattering a foot of polar crystals among the islands and nearby shores. When the last low clouds scudded out to sea, everything was wrapped in soft contours of blinding white; and in the days that followed, cobalt blue polar air cascaded down upon the coast and rimed the shores in grinning white lips of ice. For three days afterward, tongues of sea smoke leapt from the vaporous air-sea surface to obscure every horizontal view on the water while fantastic gauzy shapes from the ice kingdoms of the north ghost-danced across the bay.

In between these massive and stupendous cold fronts that rattle the bones of the dead, maritime air masses begin to shift uneasily about, pushing damp-cool or dry-cold air from place to place as the jet stream slats about in the upper atmosphere, jumping from one latitudinal groove to another. This year, by the second week of January, no one could fail to notice an un-winterly pattern caused by the deflection of the jet stream far to the south of its normal location. Not just along the Maine archipelago, but throughout the entire Northeast, a progression of warm fronts broke winter's back early. Changes in latitudes; changes in attitudes.

Meteorologists point out that the jet stream oscillation can be traced to cyclical events a half a world away where equatorial trade winds periodically rearrange Pacific ocean currents and cause what fishermen call "El Nino," heralding a catastrophic drop in fish landings. But here on the Maine coast, a warmer winter means higher landings for inshore boats, lower fuel bills, more money, less flu, improved mental health, and generally lower levels of cabin fever for grown-ups. But it also means more rain than snow, a winter mud season, less skiing, more frustration for kids, fewer snowy owls, and higher-than-average snowmobile losses on thin ice. It's hard to know what to hope for, exactly, except when you cast the ice-stiffened lines off a wharf and point the bow toward the low rim of an island on the smudgy horizon; and then you are unmitigatedly relieved for winter's respite.

On January 18, Peter Ralston, Lisa Shields and I travel to Bass Harbor to pick up RAVEN at Bass Harbor Boat where Chummy Rich and his crew have been upgrading a number of her systems to increase her handiness and the margins that accompany winter's work.

From there we steam over to the F. W. Rich wharf to fuel up. Just around Lopus Point, we can see two shrimp boats and several re-rigged lobster boats dragging for scallops. Mo Rich is waiting for their return and laconically remarks that both the supply and prices are holding up, except for the mysterious "blue" scallops that

Peter Ralston, RAVEN's skipper, at the helm

have been showing up from some locales, such as those down off the "Spoons." Blue scallops are a harmless alteration of unknown origin in the color of our favorite bivalve adductor muscle, but the weird color renders them un-marketable.

We head out across Bass Harbor Bar, where a flood tide and easterly wind have driven up a steep and opposing sea. RAVEN's bow rises to meet each new wall of water and her hull shudders momentarily with each sharp crest, while green water piles around the pilothouse; but the deep and steady pulse of the new Caterpillar diesel gives an unusual sense of security across this narrow piece of unfriendly water. We steam up the Western Way into a world of rounded grayness with all of Mount Desert's mountains arrayed on a foreshortened horizon before entering Great Cranberry's rolling harbor. We are here to deliver ballots for elections of board members to the Great Cranberry Futures Group, which islanders have organized as a forum to discuss community development strategies. The by-laws of the organization call for a slate of four year-round islanders and three seasonal residents, but everyone is surprised and pleased that 25 volunteers have agreed to run for election, an important sign of community commitment and hopefulness.

As darkness draws in, the wind is still building from the raw easterly quadrant. We weather the tip of Long Point on our way to a more protected berth in Islesford's harbor. Over the radio, lobsterman and Cranberry Isles selectman Dave Thomas guides us to a mooring and we row into the Co-op wharf. Dave, his wife, Cindy, and their two daughters have kindly invited us to dinner. We climb into his pickup and spend the

evening sharing island news from along the archipelago. Like many lobstermen on the Maine coast, Dave is spending the winter ashore repairing traps and the like, after what we have heard was a record fall lobster run, not only here but along a vast section of the midcoast. Although the harbor is a little less active than normal, it's reassuring to know that the hard-shelled mainstay of Maine island life is not only alive, but has been increasingly steadily during the past four to five years.

The next morning, after meeting with *Inter-Island News* correspondent Ted Spurling, we head out to Frenchboro to pick up Jim Wilmerding, Island Schools director, where he has spent the night. Because the state ferry service makes just two brief stops per week on Frenchboro, Jim's and everyone's arrivals and departures have to be carefully planned. The entire contingent of Frenchboro scholars, along with their teacher, tumble out of the schoolhouse and come down to the wharf to greet us and see Jim off. Of all of the 15 year-round island communities, no other appears more at risk than Frenchboro's, now that several more islanders have made the decision to move ashore. Tina Lunt, one of the islanders who wants to stay, along with her husband, Danny, and their two boys, Zachary and Nathaniel, is stoic, but it is emotionally difficult to weave the kind of ties that bind a community together when, in spite of determined efforts to attract new settlers, the number who can carve out a life here keeps dwindling.

Soon RAVEN pokes back out into exposed waters for the short trip across to Burnt Coat Harbor on Swan's Island. We swing by the new salmon farm lease area between Scrag and Harbor Islands where Mike Camber and Tommy Rydell are finishing the morning feeding. Mike tells us with obvious relief that water temperatures are still near 5 degrees Celsius (41 degrees Fahrenheit), since it means that the salmon are still feeding well. Last year at this time, sea temperatures had already plummeted to zero and Mike, Tommy, Sonny Sprague and everyone else connected with the Island Aquaculture Company held their collective breaths as the farm narrowly escaped a lethal superchill. Although no one wants to tempt fate, a few more weeks of this climatic interval will mean that the sea temperature cannot fall to fatal levels. The major problem with the farm right now, says Mike, is that the "farmers" have underestimated the amount of feed the salmon would consume during the warm fall and winter, which is a comparatively good problem to have since the fish have outgrown the projections.

When we get into Burnt Coat Harbor and tie up in Minturn at the processing plant, school board member Candy Joyce comes down to pick up Jim to take him to the school while Lisa meets with selectman Dexter Lee regarding a proposed zoning ordinance limiting the height of cellular towers on the island. Peter Ralston meanwhile has a date with Galen and Ted Turner to photograph their extraordinary collection of Swan's Island's maritime history (see p. 42).

Left briefly to my own devices, I flip through RAVEN's log and read backwards through the fall, summer and spring recalling a sampling of her voyages carrying Lisa Shields and Jim Wilmerding and other Institute staff to support a wide variety of efforts along the archipelago.

November 1: To North Haven to pick up retired ferry captain Dick Shields, then to Northeast Harbor to meet Lisa, who has come from a different direction, then to Great Cranberry for a meeting to discuss the future of the island and fate of one of its wharves.

RAVEN at Monhegan

October 18-20: To Monhegan in light northerly air to pick up school children for the small schools conference, then to Matinicus. Spent the night in Criehaven Harbor; dinner with lobsterman, Anson Norton. Next day to Isle au Haut.

September 6-7: To North Haven to pick up Lisa, then to Bass Harbor to pick up Jim then to Frenchboro for an evening school board meeting (which reconvenes the next morning), then to Swan's for Jim's visit to the school and Lisa's meeting with Sonny Sprague regarding the proposed cod and haddock hatchery. Return to Rockland by 6:30 p.m.

August 25-27: To Russ Island to survey a season of use of this Institute island, then to Webb Cove to walk the boundaries of the Settlement Quarry, an important piece of Stonington's working waterfront which is advertised for a public auction. Then to Criehaven with Annette Naegel (Science and Stewardship Director) for an evening with the community to celebrate (among other things) the Army Corps of Engineers agreement to rebuild the island breakwater, originally damaged in 1978.

August 15-16: To Boothbay Harbor for a meeting with members of the Boothbay Harbor Regional Land Trust regarding their recent acquisition of a critical piece of land at Ovensmouth, their interest in Indiantown Island, the future of nesting colonies on Outer White, Fisherman and Lower Mark islands.

August 11: To Cow Island to meet with the owner, then to Black and Hungry Islands to survey part of a season's use on these Institute-owned islands.

August 10: To Southern Island, then to Allen and Benner Islands, then to Broad Cove for an unforgettable dinner of fresh striped bass from the Kennebec (47 inches), new potatoes from Cushing, sweet corn from Union and Maine island blueberry pie.

August 6: To Whitehead Island for inspection of lighthouse keepers' buildings proposed (along with 32 other lighthouse properties) for federal transfer to the Institute, before being turned over to local towns, state agencies and non-profits. Meeting with Dave Gamage and Pat Currier, who have painstakingly tended the Whitehead buildings for so long in an astonishing show of pure volunteerism.

July 28: To a Merchant Row island generously lent for a strategic planning retreat of Institute staff to discuss organizational challenges confronting us as we approach our second decade of growth and service along the archipelago.

June 28-29: To Bass Harbor and Northeast Harbor to attend friend and Institute trustee Hank Neilson's memorial service; a sad day for the coast of Maine.

June 10-11: To Seal Bay, Vinalhaven, for Institute trustees meeting.

May 31-June 1: To Casco Bay, with Jim Wilmerding, Island Schools director, for visits to Chebeague, Long and Cliff, but steady and powerful winds (35-45 SW) necessitated a stopover at Pentecost Harbor, Allen Island, when the pounding became too great. Responded to a Mayday off Monhegan (sailing vessel FRIENDSHIP), tried to help but couldn't make way, nor could Capt. Jim Barstow aboard his LAURA B. Ran into Port Clyde, but too rough for a mooring, and then to Maple Juice Cove for the night. The following day, with more wind promised, headed back to Rockland.

May 17-20: Pick up RAVEN in Bass Harbor with her new 3116 Caterpillar diesel and head to Rockland to pick up staff. Disconnect fuel vents which are taking on water and causing problems, then proceed to Monhegan for first leg of small schools conference. Spent night on Monhegan, then left with two students and teacher and ran down to Frenchboro to deliver them to the island schools gathering. The next day to Islesford for 12 kids and three adults and back to Frenchboro where water in the fuel shut us down. Chummy Rich from Bass Harbor Boat came out to help sort out the problem; into Bass Harbor for filters and back to Frenchboro for evening festivities.

The reading of RAVEN's log, as recorded by her captain, Peter Ralston, gives a broad sweep of her journeys east and west along this long, linear, obstinate, intricate, convoluted, wondrous coast. But I have also brought along the journal I keep as first mate, foredeckman and galley crew to refresh the memory of other journeys, not just aboard RAVEN, but on the Institute's other boats, FISH HAWK and SANDERLING.

One entry, in particular, recalls something of fall's glory gone. The Institute's Annual Conference is to be held in Castine at the Maine Maritime Academy, having outgrown the facilities on Hurricane Island. Peter Ralston and I decide to use the opportunity to take RAVEN up the Penobscot River to Bangor, the head of tide, before ending up in Castine. In all of our easting and westing, we've never made the trip to the head of tide in our own backyard, and the tides are just right to catch the morning flood that will carry

FISH HAWK is scheduled for structural and cosmetic work this year.

us to the innermost parts of the Penobscot estuary and back down again like a willful piece of flotsam. Besides, it's time, perhaps past time, to survey the connections between the bay, the islands, the river and her mills.

October 18: 5:30 a.m., Rockland Harbor. Venus, low in the east, the morning star, is the only bright light in the sky, while the faint glow of rosy-fingered dawn begins to stroke the sleeping breast of the bay. The flickering eye of Brown's Head is far off the bow as we come abeam the Breakwater Light and head into the red-rimmed light of dawn, watching while autumn's slanting easterly rays slowly pull a shade up on the crimson flanks of the Camden Hills. Just a blackbird shy of "Morning Has Broken."

The bay begins to narrow noticeably at Northport where ancient metamorphic rocks tumble from the land's massive shoulders to the edge of the water. Saturday Cove is the smallest dent in the armament of the bay, but a few hopeful vessels still cling to their moorings in the deeply shadowed light. Belfast is off to port, as we head for the shores of Sears Island to see up close the existing cargo port at Mack Point and the site for a new one proposed for the western shore of this uninhabited 900-acre island.

It's 7 a.m. when we round up into Long Cove; Mack Point is off the bow, the white clapboards and steeples of Searsport are off our port quarter. We steam by the oak- and spruce-lined shores of Sears Island, passing over the dredged ship channel which terminates at Mack Point. We poke slowly up into Long Cove; with the tide still running out, we can't go too far in, but there's not much evidence of activity here. In fact it would be a surprise to see a flock of shorebirds wheel by on the wing, or watch a great blue heron stalk shadows on these 60 acres of tidal flats or a seal's surprise surface; this is, after all, an industrial site, but not even a herring gull stirs here, a lasting legacy of a 5,000-gallon fuel spill back in the 1970s that has never been cleaned up. Although no one knows for sure (because

no one has bothered to ask), it appears that the effects of this spill continue to exert a chronic, low-level, toxic stress, which you'd expect would hit particularly hard on creatures at the bottom of the marine food chain. There's so little life in the cove because it's sick and there's no food.

There's also a dearth of activity at the long finger pier of the Bangor and Aroostook Railroad, which has a dilapidated, faded and outdated look to it. This pier is in fact part of the *raison d'être* for construction on Sears Island, because it so obviously needs to be replaced, but planners have long maintained that Mack Point lacks the space, orientation and compatibility with existing operations to rebuild here. Only a new port will do. At the next pier over, a single man is up in the steel superstructure, and we exchange waves while he waits for his ship — any ship — to come in, seemingly in limbo until a decision is reached on whether to invest another $65 to $80 million out of the public pocket to build a modern, efficient cargo port a mere stone's throw away on the wild shores of Sears Island.

Although we have not spent any real time exploring here, a few things seem obvious. First, Mack Point is hardly the kind of cargo port most people would like to think operates at the head of Penobscot Bay to instill confidence that it can safely handle the coal and oil that comes in here, Sears Island or no Sears Island. Second, the lack of a strategy to monitor the effects of the existing source of pollution in Long Cove strains the credibility of those who say that all the environmental issues in the lengthy Sears Island debate have already been addressed. Third, although using 200 of Sears Island's 900 acres for a new cargo port won't be an ecological catastrophe in and of itself, this is an old-style development model: take a chunk of virgin territory for a new facility and turn a blind eye to the decaying infrastructure staring you in the face.

(continued on page 90)

THE GULF OF MAINE

A Mirror for the World's Oceans

FOUR HUNDRED MILES from end to end, the Gulf of Maine spans states, provinces, an international boundary and several distinct cultures. Near its southwest extremity is Boston, which first prospered two centuries ago because of its magnificent harbor and easy access to a fabulous supply of fish and shellfish. From its beginnings as a port, Boston became an economic, political, social and cultural center; today Boston is the place where the Gulf of Maine, New England and the United States' northeastern megalopolis all meet. The gilded cod atop its statehouse dome has become an international metaphor for marine sustainability.

At the other end of the gulf is the Bay of Fundy, best known for its immense tides. To residents of the United States, Fundy seems remote, wild, almost Arctic in character, populated largely by exotic seabirds and whales. In fact, this region has a history of settlement as long as New England's — occupied first by Native American fishermen, then by Europeans who came in search of fish, timber and opportunities to trade. Today the Canadian communities that ring the Bay of Fundy have their differences — Saint John is a port whose tonnage rivals Portland and Boston, while Campobello, Truro and Yarmouth all depend on fishing and tourism — but they share a critical part of the Gulf of Maine. Like Boston, they are places where the inland and maritime aspects of this great region come together.

"The Gulf of Maine is a microcosm," former Maine Senator George Mitchell told participants in the Island Institute's Annual Conference last October. It "mirrors in smaller detail most of the problems reflected in the wide world's experience of oceanic degradation." Like oceans everywhere, the gulf and its watershed are prey to toxins, over-fishing, sewage discharges, the destruction of its wetlands, the over-exploitation of upland forests — in short, all the problems we humans cause when we concentrate ourselves along coastlines, as we must to live.

Yet as Mitchell pointed out, we in this region have reason to be hopeful. The Gulf of Maine is not yet as polluted as other bodies of water; lessons learned in Chesapeake Bay and elsewhere can be applied to the gulf before it is too late. "What's needed," the former senator said, "is an approach that crosses manmade political boundaries to bring together the needs the gulf serves for the communities that live along its shores."

For a region just beginning to sense the dimensions of its shared identity, his message could not be more timely and important.

— David D. Platt

Jack McConnell photo

"THE OCEAN IS OUR COMMON BIRTHPLACE"

"Children have learned from parents about the seas and the fish."

"I believe in an environment that includes the work and existence of human beings."

Remarks by former Senator George Mitchell at the Annual Conference of the Island Institute, October 15, 1994

MANY THINGS set Maine apart from the rest of the nation. One of the most obvious is the more than 3,500 islands that dot our coastline. Over the past 11 years, the Island Institute has worked to highlight these islands and their year-round population, and to bring attention to the economic, cultural and ecological heritage they represent. I commend the Island Institute's many efforts.

I support the Maine Lights Program, which represents an innovative approach to preserving 33 Maine lighthouses. If successful, it could become a model for the appropriate transfer of lighthouses from the Coast Guard to local communities all across the country, and I look forward to coming back to a future conference when the program is a reality.

Although this program has been an important focus this year, it has, of course, not been the only focus. We have each continued in our work to preserve our coastal environment and heritage, through both educational and legislative efforts.

Learning to live with the natural world is a lifetime process, and each piece of information we learn reveals the many pieces we do not know.

One of the largest pieces of that puzzle, and a piece we have only begun to understand in dim outline, is the role of the oceans.

THE VALUE OF THE COASTS

The world's oceans contain about 97 percent of all the water on our planet. The oceans are the world's most important factor in climate control. They absorb much of the sun's heat and redistribute it from the Equator to the Poles. In the process they moderate the climates of continents like Europe and North America and nations like Japan.

One-third of the world's population lives within 37 miles of a coastline. Many millions more live within an easy day's travel of coastlines. The majority of the earth's 5.5 billion people live around the coastal fringes of the continents.

Coastal environments, whether tropical mangrove swamps, tidal flats, marshes or estuaries, are, biologically, the richest parts of the oceans. They are feeding and nursery grounds for more than 90 percent of fish, including fish that spend their adult lives in the open seas. Almost 99 percent of commercially valuable fish are caught within 200 miles of a coastline. Coastal environments are enormous sanctuaries for migratory birds.

They are catchment areas for river sediments that would be dispersed in the oceans if they were not trapped by marsh grasses and other plants.

Human settlement and its density have already taken a toll on our planet's coasts. Many of the world's large coastal cities don't have wastewater treatment, and spill raw sewage directly into the oceans.

It's estimated that half of all tropical mangrove swamps have been destroyed by development.

The collapse of the New England fishery isn't a local phenomenon. It reflects a worldwide phenomenon, one whose full effects are becoming apparent only now.

FISHING: A WORLDWIDE CRISIS

During the postwar decades of the 1950s and 1960s, global saltwater fish landings tripled to 60 million metric tons, worldwide, as a result of improved commercial fishing technologies, the drive to gather more food, and the sheer growth of population. In the 1970s and 1980s, fish landings rose but more slowly. They peaked at 86 million metric tons in 1989.

In those decades, enormous changes took place in commercial fishing practices. The use of satellites, directional sonar and spotter planes helped fishermen find and net huge shoals of pelagic fish in the open seas, the Peruvian anchovies, the Japanese and south American sardine varieties, the Alaskan pollock. Factory ships that processed the catch at sea and didn't need to return to shore for many weeks at a time made enormous driftnet excursions commercially feasible. Driftnets that cover five to 50 kilometers of ocean at a time, trapping everything in their path, were dragged in all the fishing waters of the world. The catch was enormous. So was the cost.

In 1986, an international agreement was reached which established 200-mile exclusive economic zones offshore. Unfortunately, it did not have the intended effect, for a number of reasons.

The first response to the 200-mile limit was the negotiation among nations for fishing rights in each others' waters.

The next reaction to the 200-mile zone — usually a political reaction in democratic countries — was putting an end to foreign fishing rights, and expanding national fishing fleets to compensate. That happened here in America as it did in virtually every fishing nation around the world.

Governments subsidized the construction of newer, more modern and more efficient fishing vessels for their own citizens, and barred from their waters the ships of other nations.

The next response, as fish landings failed to increase in pace with expanded, more efficient fleets, was the exploitation of secondary species prized by the Japanese and others to maintain income and make up for falling groundfish catches.

"Clam harvests in Downeast Maine declined from 4.6 million lbs. in 1982 to 500,000 lbs. in 1993."

The fourth factor was the effort to manage the fisheries scientifically. It varied widely. But overall, the first attempt at management failed. The result can be seen in the outcomes.

In 1968, Atlantic cod landings totaled 800,000 metric tons. But in 1991, a managed catch of 50,000 tons was all that could be permitted. Canada has shut down its cod fishery entirely. North Sea cod spawning stocks have dwindled to 66,000 metric tons, about a third of what the U.N. judges to be a sustainable level.

There are about three million fishing vessels in the world today. But it's estimated that Europe and Iceland could reduce their fleets by 40 percent without reducing the commercial catch at all. The difficulty is to find a fair way to do that. Europe hasn't discovered it yet and neither has anyone else.

People have wrested a living from the sea for centuries. If they are going to keep on doing so, we will have to pay more attention to the oceans than we have in the past.

CONSEQUENCES

Paying attention to the oceans means paying attention to the entire environment because the oceans are a huge and integral part of the environment.

What we can say with some certainty is that global warming would shift oceanic currents. We cannot yet know where or how, but we do know that as ocean currents shift, prevailing winds will shift, temperatures above warm currents will shift with the currents and colder temperatures will become prevalent where the moderating effects of those ocean currents are lost.

Other effects of climate change could be just as dramatic.

THE GULF OF MAINE

Here in the United States, attention has focused on our coastlines only sporadically as we have worked to clean up polluted air, rivers and lakes. But I'm pleased to say that one of the places where the process of study, pollution control and abatement is taking place is the Gulf of Maine.

The Gulf of Maine covers a vast area that includes open ocean as well as islands, bays, harbors and estuarine environments. It has historically been a rich fishery and therefore a richly diverse biological environment. It has also been subjected to the kinds of unmanaged development that have taken a toll on all the world's coastal regions.

The Gulf of Maine region includes the watershed that contributes so much of the sedimentation and pollution to which it is subjected.

(continued on page 89)

RIVER TOWN, BOOM TOWN, ISLAND ENCLAVE

Three Penobscot Bay communities face their future by understanding their common past

BOB MOORE

Jeff Dworsky

*This past year, a steering committee organized by the Island Institute and others undertook a study of Penobscot Bay and its watershed, in hopes of increasing residents' awareness of their region and the connections between a healthy bay and a strong economy. The Institute will publish **State of the Bay** later this year documenting the region's human and natural resources. In essence, the report will be a "snapshot" of the region in 1995, including enough historical material to make comparisons with the region as it was in the past.*

*The three community profiles included here will appear in **State of the Bay**, along with information about the rest of the region, a set of economic, social and environmental "trend indicators," and a bibliography of scientific studies undertaken in the bay region in recent years.*

WHEN EUROPEANS first settled the Penobscot Bay region, they set patterns that are reflected in how life is lived there today. They needed sheltered harbors, timber and other natural resources, good farmland, sites for water-powered mills, transportation access to the interior and the sea. The Penobscot River and the islands in the bay answered many of these needs, and many of the communities established by early settlers survive to this day.

Changing requirements brought prosperity to some towns and hard times to others. Seaborne commerce made island settlements more viable in the 19th century than they are today. Lumber and location transformed Bangor into a boom town around the time of the Civil War. But when circumstances changed — when railroads and highways gave the mainland an advantage over islands, for example, or when northern Maine's first timber crop ran out and other sources became available — these communities were forced to adapt. The following brief profiles of three communities in the Penobscot Bay region describe how each survived enormous transitions in its own very individual way.

The communities have changed completely since they were settled, and they are very different from one another today. Yet, situated as they are in Penobscot Bay, they share a common sense of place. The Penobscot River and the bay played a significant role in each community from the beginning. In one case (Bangor) the city eventually turned its back on the river, acknowledging it only as a place to discharge waste. Inevitably, however, the forces that drew people to settle on the shores of Penobscot Bay and the river have triumphed, and today all three communities have come to appreciate their location in the Penobscot Bay watershed.

Situated on the southern tip of Deer Isle, Stonington is doing all it can to make fishing last as a way of life.

BANGOR

PERCHED AT THE HEAD of tide on the Penobscot River, Bangor has always had a strong physical and cultural connection to Penobscot Bay, 30 miles downstream. Until the advent of rail, and later, highway transportation, the Penobscot River provided the primary link between communities along its banks, and between the wealth of the great interior forests of Maine and the rest of the world. The Penobscot carried logs down to mills in Bangor, where they were sawed into lumber and exported from the port of Bangor. From the mid to late 19th century, millions of board feet of lumber were exported from lumber mills operating in the Bangor area to coastal cities around the world. Bangor was also a cargo and passenger port until the 1950s when railroads supplanted river traffic.

Bangor spent her youth as a booming lumber town, cosmopolitan from her connection to the world as an international port of call for steamship traffic, at the same time rowdy, often seamy, from the rough-and-tumble crews that came in with the great log drives.

Bangor has grown up and changed significantly since its 19th-century lumbering days, and while the log drives have disappeared, the city remains the cultural and economic hub for eastern, northern and central Maine. Today Bangor's ties to the expansive region it serves are stronger than ever, testimony to the city's adaptability and resourcefulness.

TROUBLE IN RIVER CITY

Throughout Bangor's history, the Penobscot River and the bay have played a significant role in the city's development. That relationship was not always a positive one for Penobscot Bay. By the time the last Penobscot log drive was over in the 1960s, Bangor had turned its back on the river. The city had become an industrial center with factories, tank farms, and mills lining the river. Rail corridors along the banks of the Penobscot further separated people from the river on both Bangor and Brewer shores. But that separation was a welcome blessing, for the river had become a polluted sewer of human and industrial waste. There was little protest over the lack of public access to a river that was for all practical purposes both ecologically and aesthetically dead. The ecological effects to the river and the bay from this industrial legacy are still being studied, but reports have shown that the sediments in the river and bay describe a plume of toxic metals and chemicals gradually decreasing in concentration along a gradient progressing into the bay.

Many of the sources of pollution have been cleaned up or eliminated, and today's discharges into the river are a small fraction of the pollution the river received in its early industrial days. Major point-sources, such as pulp and paper mills and sewage treatment plants, have

13

In the 1850s, Bangor was the world's leading lumber port and in the next two decades was second only to Chicago. In 1872, Bangor handled nearly 250 million board feet.

significantly improved the quality of their wastewater before it reaches their outfalls in the river. Stormwater runoff from urban and rural areas today accounts for a majority of the pollution entering the river, which, because of the diffuse nature of the sources, makes targeting cleanup a challenge. The fact that water quality in the river continues to improve, even while bordered by a metropolitan area with a large industrial and manufacturing base and a regional population of 100,000, leaves hope for further improvement.

A REGIONAL DOWNTOWN

As a job center, Bangor is the largest in eastern Maine. With a resident population of 33,000 and a metropolitan population of 81,000, Bangor has a large workforce from which to draw. The Bangor area's labor force of 48,000 is the highest concentration in Maine outside of Portland. To entice new businesses to locate there, the Bangor Chamber of Commerce promotes the city's sprawling regional influence over three market sectors. The first serves 28 communities closest to Bangor, an area with a population of 96,000 and extending 40 miles from Winterport on the south to Charleston on the northwest side of the city.

The second market area claims a six-county area in central, eastern and northern Maine, and includes a population of 350,000 people. Michael Bush of the Eastern Maine Development District, a private non-profit development group in Bangor, ascribes Bangor's role as a regional center as a natural outgrowth of the city's historical regional dominance during the lumber era. In what Bush describes as the "agglomeration theory" of growth, as activities become congregated, they tend to become more congregated. "The area is so dispersed," says Bush, "that Bangor has become the commercial gateway to the western mountains, Baxter State Park, Acadia National Park, the Downeast region of Maine and Canada." Thus, for

medical, financial or legal services, a person from Greenville, Machias or Canada might travel as far as Bangor. While in the area, they might take advantage of the greater variety of services and retail shopping and restaurant choices in Bangor that they don't have in their home territory.

Serving such a broad geographic area has the reciprocal effect of making Bangor vulnerable to economic fluctuations there: if the outlying communities are economically depressed, people would be less likely to travel to Bangor to spend their money. "The economic health of the entire region, from Aroostook County to Waterville and Augusta to Hancock and Washington Counties, has a big impact on the vibrancy of Bangor as a regional center," says Bush, describing the fragile balance between Bangor and its outlying communities. "Bangor wouldn't be Bangor if didn't have a large number of people commuting in from other areas. If they don't have a healthy economy there, it'll hurt Bangor." This is less true for coastal Maine, says Bush, because people from away tend to migrate there, often wealthy people with retirement incomes. Those patterns of migration are not reflected in Bangor's hinterlands.

What the chamber of commerce describes as Bangor's tertiary market reaches out as far as the provinces of New Brunswick and Quebec. But Canadian shoppers, formerly a strong source of retail trade in Bangor, have recently disappeared, kept away by the low value of the U.S. dollar and by the fact that the Canadian government started collecting 9 percent provincial tax at the border, making Maine products less of a bargain than they used to be. Bush says the decrease in Canadian business has had a noticeable impact on Bangor's retail economy.

Bangor's rise as the dominant regional center has supplanted the role of smaller regional communities in eastern Maine such as Machias, Dover-Foxcroft and

Calais. "They didn't have the critical mass," says Bush. Now, because Bangor offers so much, it will be more difficult for these formerly strong town centers to come back.

HERE WE GROW AGAIN

Perhaps Bangor's biggest strength is that the largest employers are less subject to major employment shifts: three hospitals, including Eastern Maine Medical Center, the second largest in the state, employing 2,444; and six colleges, including the University of Maine in Orono, which employs 2,500. According to the Bangor Chamber of Commerce, the 48,000-member metropolitan labor force works in 26,000 retail and service jobs, including 10,000 local, state and federal government jobs. Far from being strictly a service economy, however, the greater Bangor area has a strong manufacturing base, employing 4,600 workers, 28 percent of whom work in paper industry jobs at Eastern Fine Paper (Brewer), James River (Old Town) and Champion International (Bucksport).

Bangor's prosperity is also dependent on the natural resources of the region. "Look at the forests — we're probably cutting too much, and polluting lakes," says Bush. "But if the solution is to stop cutting, look at the probable impact it would have on the forest and paper industries. Go north to Old Town, Lincoln and Millinocket. Without those jobs, the whole region will collapse. The retail and service sectors in Bangor would be devastated if the big employers shut down."

Bangor has room to spread out and a city hall with an aggressive intent to pursue growth. The city capitalized on the problematic closure of Dow Air Force Base in the late 1960s by developing Bangor's niche as an international airline refueling and customs stop-over. When the base first closed, the city's population dropped 21 percent, from 38 to 30 thousand. Stan Moses of the Bangor Office of Planning and Community Development says, "Now cities across the U.S. facing base closures are being directed to Bangor to ask, 'How did you do it?'"

Moses answers: "It took 25 years and a significant amount of planning to make the base area a busy commercial section of the city."

Being the downtown to a population as spread out as eastern Maine's has its disadvantages, however. As a "central city," Bangor attracts regional enterprises such as non-profit organizations, hospitals, schools, churches, universities and colleges. The downside is that the city provides water, sewer, fire and police protection to these institutions without being able to tax them, and financing those services is a big problem for the city. Stan Moses uses the sewer system as a case in point. The city recently constructed a $22-million secondary sewage treatment facility to comply with the federal Clean Water Act. "Over the last five or six years, sewer

Bangor's relationship to the Penobscot River changed with the decline of shipping, and for years the river served chiefly to carry away the city's wastes. Today's revived waterfront is home to pleasure craft, but compared with the vessels of lumber-shipping days, their numbers are few.

STONINGTON

WALKING THROUGH STONINGTON on a bright, cold December day, you're likely to see vehicles parked along the street with license plates from both coasts of the United States. The people driving them aren't the typical camera-toting tourists normally seen jaywalking local streets in the summer. Stonington hasn't become a year-round tourist resort town — far from it. The newcomers are urchin divers and their crews, come to Stonington to capitalize on the opportunity to supply the Japanese with urchin roe.

For Stonington it's only the latest boom. At the turn of the century, Stonington granite was a global commodity, quarried on local shores and islands and shipped to cities worldwide. By 1910, the local population had swelled to 2,038 and consisted largely of immigrant stoneworkers whose descendants still remain in the area. Today, only a handful of stoneworkers are employed in Stonington and nearby Crotch Island. Stonington's population of 1,252 reflects a gradual decline that even the current economy, based on fishing, has been unable to stem. And signs are evident that fisheries are becoming a risky vocation even for the most steadfast fishermen in Stonington.

Situated on the southern tip of Deer Isle, Stonington is doing all it can to make fishing last as a way of life. In the face of declining groundfish stocks, the Stonington fishing fleet has had to be flexible, making the transition from the cod and haddock fishery to scalloping and lobstering, and now sea urchins.

A TRADITIONAL FISHING TOWN

The number of fishing boats using the Stonington Fish Pier provides a measure of fishing's predominance in Stonington's economy: in 1986, the then-new Fish Pier served 65 boats. Today, that number is up to 103 boats, a 58 percent increase. It is significant to note that not a single recreational boat uses the pier. "The pier's a godsend," says lobsterman Brent Jones. "But now there are too many urchin buyers underfoot. A lobsterman can't haul his traps out with all of them crawling around."

Traditionally a small-boat fleet, Stonington has been able to adapt to emerging fisheries like urchins and, more recently, sea cucumbers. Constructed in the mid 1980s, the pier enhanced fishermen's access to buyers who bid competitively for their catch. It changed the traditional relationship between fishermen and their buyers, who usually ran their own dock, provided bait and set prices for the catch.

Competition for space at the pier at least indicates a robust catch being brought in, and the town is proposing to expand the pier to accommodate more traffic.

---

user fees have gone up 10 percent every time the bills go out to customers," says Moses.

"The Bangor downtown still has its problems," says Ken Gibbs of the planning department. "Only 10 percent of the Bangor workforce works downtown. There are still a lot of empty shops, and downtown is not the economic force it used to be." The key, says Gibbs, is to "keep up with the infrastructure," to make it as attractive as possible. That means dealing with some of what Gibbs calls Bangor's "albatrosses" — enormous, empty retail stores occupying much of the downtown, but unable to bring in revenue.

RE-ESTABLISHING THE BANGOR/PENOBSCOT CONNECTION

Moses and others recognize that reconnecting the city to its waterfront encourages the perception of a better quality of life in the city. To that end, Bangor acquired a quarter-mile stretch of industrial shoreline that included a railroad switching yard, shoe factory, tank farm, coal yard, paper company and warehouse. In the early 1980s, these industrial facilities were functionally obsolete barriers to the river. "Economic times were changing, and the city had the opportunity to regain control of the waterfront and give it back to citizens of the region," says Moses. Bangor cleaned out the contaminated soil, removed the warehouses,

established a waterfront park and replaced an industrial waterfront wasteland with public open space downtown.

It helps that the Penobscot itself has improved: there is no smell, and eel fishermen and bald eagles share the river, something few cities can boast. The money spent to clean up the river by building the new secondary treatment plant has awakened interest in the river as a recreational resource, and the city has improved access for pedestrians and boaters. "Rather than see the river as a barrier between two cities, the Penobscot River and bay are important to the region in so many different ways," says Moses. Aside from the waterfront acquisitions, there is ample evidence of this awakening in Bangor: a riverside trail along the Kenduskeag Stream leading into Bangor, protected with conservation easements along both sides, follows steep wooded banks into the city from the northwest. In reviewing new development, the city focused on opening visual and physical access to the river, to the point that now the river is visible from the center of busy downtown.

"Quality of life is one of the main advantages Maine has to offer long-range, you have to preserve the natural environment," says Moses, reflecting on the city's expense and effort to improve water quality in the river. "Comparing the cost of contaminating something and the cost of cleanup, it's a lot easier to keep it clean."

Late in the 19th century, Stonington depended on both granite quarrying and fishing.

Deer Isle Historical Society (2)

Much of present-day Stonington was built around the turn of the century.

WORKING HARD, WORKING SMART

Economic booms are often followed by busts. For now, Stonington fishermen are depending on the strong work ethic that has kept them going through hard times in the past. "You're only going to die once," says Jones, adding that its preferable to work harder doing what you like than to give up and do something else. With his bait and fuel expenses on the rise, Jones sees his margins narrowing. "Then your engine up and quits," says Jones, with hardly a hint of despair. "It's part of goin' fishin' — you think you're making a living, but you never do."

Skip Greenlaw, who runs the Stonington Lobster Co-op, sees the fisherman's work ethic as something to admire while at the same time questioning whether working longer and harder is enough. He has a saying: "It's no longer enough to work hard, you have to work smart."

THE THIRD BOOM CYCLE

Waves come in sets of three, and quarrying and fishing represent the first two transition periods in the life of Stonington since 1900. The third wave came ashore in the 1980s, when the real estate frenzy that swept across Maine hit Stonington like a tidal wave. Within four years in the latter part of the decade, Stonington housing prices rose 66 percent. Waterfront property and houses with views of the harbor sold to newcomers, primarily for seasonal use. "Year-round residents are relegated to living along interior roads in town," says Nat Barrows, proprietor of the Penobscot Bay Press, which publishes three weekly newspapers for towns in east Penobscot Bay, including Stonington. "People here get frustrated by flocks of tourists in the summer," says Barrows, referring to the traffic of sea kayakers, sailors and windjammers descending on the town, and the visitors heading for Isle au Haut. "But," he adds, "the population of the island drops by half in the winter." The Stonington comprehensive plan refers to a "ghost town" effect, created when neighborhoods empty out in the fall as summer folk head home.

Still, the new arrivals to Stonington have integrated themselves into the community fairly well, according to George St. Amand, who runs Green's Landing Realty in town (named after the original settlement that became Stonington). "It's a different kind of person that's come here," says St. Amand. "They like the simplicity here. They're not trying to generate a tourist flow of traffic, like Cape Cod or the strip heading toward Mount Desert Island. They are willing to role up their sleeves and participate in town life. Sometimes overzealous, wanting things to change faster, but meshing with the native population."

Barrows notices two types of tourists in Stonington. The first type is the summer resident, or the vacationer who comes to stay for a few weeks or a month. The second type is the day-tripper. Since motels, parking, gift shops and restaurants on the island are few, so are day-trippers.

One reason there will be few additions to the short list of amenities for day-trippers is the lack of space to put them in the crowded Stonington downtown area. To make growth more complicated, the town just completed installing a $3-million sewer for the downtown area that was designed to handle only existing capacity, so future construction in town must locate its own means of sewage treatment. (Constructing the sewer through Stonington posed a challenge, because a large portion of the line had to be blasted into ledge. "Practically every house had to be set back on its foundation," remarked one local.)

DRY GULCH

A third deterrent to Stonington's becoming a tourist destination, next to space and development restrictions, is the fact that Stonington is a dry town. Town manager Roger Stone is deadpan when he remarks that there is not much push to develop Stonington. Ask him what the biggest change in Stonington has been recently, he'll say it was tarring the airfield. "I don't have people pounding the door of the town office down," says Stone. "When they come, I point out the restrictions of sewer, space and alcohol. I'd rather promote fishing and more traditional businesses, as long as they're viable."

How long traditional employment sectors remain viable is a key question for Stonington. In a trend that began during the same period as the 1980s real estate boom and still continues today, traditional fishing industry employment dropped off 10.9 percent, with a 5.1 percent decline in processing, handling, and labor jobs (the latter related to boat hands and the shutdown of the sardine processing plant in town). The Stonington economy is still very heavily dependent on the industry, with 16 percent employed in fishing, compared to 5.7 percent for Hancock County and 2.8 percent for Maine as a whole. But at the same time that traditional jobs were declining, new sectors of the area economy expanded. The number of professional

Jeff Dworsky (4)

January

Lobsterboat races

July 4

In the face of declining groundfish stocks, the Stonington fishing fleet has had to be flexible, making the transition from the cod and haddock fishery to scalloping and lobstering, and now sea urchins.

specialty occupations grew by 9.1 percent, the number of service jobs grew by 5 percent. A new medical care facility and the Haystack Mountain School of Crafts are drawing professionals and artists to the area.

AN UNEASY PROSPERITY

There is an uneasy sense in Stonington that fishing can't last the way it is forever. Skip Greenlaw had his best year ever in 1994, and he is not alone in his worry that fishing is a bubble about to burst. "There are too many people in lobstering already," says Greenlaw, echoing a sentiment around the harbor that lobstering won't be as good for long if fishing pressure increases. More and more groundfishermen are switching to lobstering, and many urchiners take to lobstering after the winter urchin harvest is over.

But sea urchins are not expected to last, especially at current harvesting rates. One day in December, Joe Grego harvested 1,090 pounds of urchins. But with 25 to 30 boats going out of Stonington for urchins, the pickings are getting harder. "You've got to jump and fetch, but there's still some out there," says Grego. "It's kind of like extreme diving out there now."

George St. Amand, whose office overlooks the Fish Pier, sees urchins going the

way of groundfish in what he likens to a harvesting frenzy. "It'd be nice if it became a reasonable, locally sustainable harvest instead of a gold rush," says St. Amand. "But now, urchin divers are coming in from all over the east and west coasts, renting houses or motel rooms for the season. They have no place to park so they park on the street, and everybody grumbles. But there's no question they do add to the economy."

HOLDING ON FOR DEAR LIFE

Diversifying the local economic base can only help Stonington residents keep their options open in the long run. Few like the idea of working in service or tourism jobs, because of the lack of opportunity for steady, year-round work in these sectors.

Fending off the trend seen on the mainland coast toward service and tourism economies, Stonington is fighting fiercely to retain its working link to the sea. With both the local population and traditional fishing employment gradually declining, the future poses big challenges to Stonington's resourcefulness in dealing with the boom and bust cycles it has always known. "The booms and busts aren't terrible," says St. Amand. "As long as people are willing to work hard, they'll survive."

St. Amand looks over the harbor out to the bay, and sees the health of Penobscot Bay playing a strong role in the life of Stonington for a long time to come. "When the lobster traps and draggers disappear, something else will come, like aquaculture. Pollution is the worst part of it."

Before the turn of the century, Islesboro had five villages scattered along its length, making convenient landings for mail and supply boats steaming from all points of Penobscot Bay.

Islesboro has come to accept and depend on its relationship with long-time summer residents.

ISLESBORO

WITH OVER 50 MILES of shoreline for only 14 square miles of island, the relationship between Islesboro and Penobscot Bay is intimate. When steamship traffic was the primary transportation link in the region, Islesboro had close ties to surrounding communities in the upper bay. The distance to the mainland communities of Northport and Lincolnville to the west, Castine and Cape Rosier to the east, and Searsport to the north is barely three miles, and Belfast, once the city center for the upper bay, lies only six miles northwest of the island.

"Islesboro always had relations with the mainland," says Ralph Gray, a long-time resident who came over from Cape Rosier when he was five years old. "The bay used to be more connected when steamers and packets ran service to Belfast, Castine and Northport. People used to go over to Belfast, which is the county seat, to do their banking or see the doctor, or over to Northport or Castine to find sweethearts." Gray recalls taking the steamship to his dentist in Belfast. "I had two sons born in the hospital there."

With the decline of steamship traffic on Penobscot Bay, the importance of proximity to these ports declined as well. It heralded a big change for Islesboro and Penobscot Bay. Traffic patterns that had for over a century flowed east and west over water began flowing north and south, connecting communities on the mainland by road. When ferry service to Lincolnville took over as the island's only access to the mainland, Islesboro's focus shifted to Camden. Islanders took their bank accounts there and conducted all their other mainland commerce on the west shore of Penobscot Bay as they still do today. "Camden was the up-and-coming town then," recalls Gray, "about the same time as Belfast was beginning to decline."

Today, Islesboro is an island community unto itself. Like Stonington and Bangor, it has experienced major transitions, except that Islesboro has come to accept and depend on its relationship with long-time summer residents. They have settled into an enduring partnership that safeguards a mutual vision of the way life on Islesboro should be.

Perhaps because of its easy access by boat, Islesboro evolved from its early roots as a fishing and agricultural community into the home of globe-spanning merchant sea captains. Before the turn of the century, Islesboro had five villages scattered along its length, making convenient landings for mail and supply boats steaming from all points of Penobscot Bay.

FANTASY ISLAND

Even bigger changes occurred on Islesboro in the 1890s, when the island became a summer haven to wealthy families from Bangor, Boston, New York and Philadelphia. They constructed summer cottages of grand proportions, which led to the evolution of Islesboro's year-round community into a caretaking role. Islesboro families began tending to the leviathan homes and grounds that required year-round attention to maintain — lawn mowing, landscaping, and the services of woodworkers, painters and plumbers. Summers brought a demand for domestics, boatmen and gardeners. So began a relationship between Islesboro residents and summer families that has varied little in 100 years.

Many people ask why Islesboro's summer homes are called "cottages" instead of a term more consistent with their size. "Because, to the people who built them, that's what they were," says Gray, who is now semi-retired from a life of caretaking Dark Harbor cottages. Tending to Islesboro's summer colony is scarcely what anyone would dare call a tourist economy — many of the same families have been coming to Islesboro for generations, and have developed loyalties to the people who work on the island. More accurately, it is a relationship ingrained in tradition on Islesboro, fully supported by all parties.

Islesboro became a magnet for East Coast society in the late 1800s. The U.S. economy was booming, and life in the Gay Nineties would have been drab if the families of corporate industrialists had to spend the summer in cities choked with foul air and water.

"What they lacked at home, they found here," says Steve Miller, Islesboro resident and director of the local land preservation group, the Islesboro Islands Trust. "They found a pristine, healthy playground where their families could enjoy clambakes, breathe clean air, learn to sail and swim, and return home after Labor Day with ruddy cheeks." Miller surmises that they may have chosen Islesboro over other surrounding communities not simply because it is an attractive setting, but because the island population was probably somewhat literate, having benefited from the worldly lifestyles of its peripatetic sea captains.

ISLAND WORK

Islesboro's year-round population of 579 is self-sustaining: 93 percent of the island work force stays on the island to work. But the fact that only eight islanders commute off Islesboro for work every day belies the nature of the island economy: far from being a bustling commercial center, workers are largely self-employed caretakers, domestics and tradesmen. On the first ferry from Lincolnville to Islesboro on a bright December morning, nearly every vehicle was a tradesman's pickup: construction, painting, electrician services. Clearly, there is work enough to go around in maintaining the summer homes on Islesboro, a broad economic base that has proven reliable in its employment potential.

In an employment survey of the island work force that the Town of Islesboro conducted in 1992, island boatyards provided the highest employment on Islesboro. After that, in descending order of importance, came employment as domestics or caretakers, at the school, as builders/contractors and painters, and finally, in fishing. Fishing accounted for half as many jobs as domestics.

LOBSTER TRAP

The recent boom times for lobstering haven't skipped the upper bay, however,

Islesboro's proximity to the mainland made it a relatively cosmopolitan place in the 19th century, before it became a destination resort for the wealthy.

Boom times are luring Islesboro residents out of caretaking, into the lobster fishery.

and lobstering is luring Islesboro residents out of caretaking. Ralph Gray is skeptical that the fishing will remain as lucrative as it is, and questions why the young men of Islesboro are so willing to make the heavy investment in boats and gear. "They're going along on this big bubble, buying $10,000 to $30,000 boats," he worries aloud. "Lobsters've always gone in cycles." Gray agrees with the popular explanation around Penobscot Bay that the absence of groundfish, and the corresponding decrease in their predation on lobster juveniles, is responsible for the boom in lobstering.

"Lobsters are back like the old-timers say they were three generations ago," says Ace Rolerson, who has a plumbing business and also runs the Island Market. Rolerson recalls local legends of times when lobsters were so plentiful that dogs would retrieve them from under the seaweed at low tide. He agrees that lobster fishing is the biggest change he has seen in Islesboro employment in recent memory. Business was brisk enough in 1994 that a Lincolnville buyer came over to Islesboro to buy the local catch and provide bait. That saved island fishermen the headache of waiting hours in the hot summer sun

for the ferry to bring their catch to the mainland, as well as the trip to Rockland to purchase bait.

Gray remains unconvinced that tradesmen are making a wise choice laying down their tools and getting into lobstering. His long experience on Islesboro has told him where dependable work resides. "Most of the island is dependent on summer people. Without them, we would have no stores, no work . . . I don't know what the hell people would do. If you were a carpenter or a painter, you counted on the summer people to keep employed. Lobsters have changed all that."

MORE SERVICES, HIGHER COSTS

At the coffee stand in the Island Market, morning traffic flows freely, as do opinions. Rolerson and others opine that another big change on Islesboro in the last decade was the growth in the Town's expenditures on infrastructure. Islanders recall the days when the Islesboro fire truck was a relic that needed to be shoveled out of the snow if the time came to use it; now the Town has a reliable machine with a roof over it to keep the weather out. Another Town expense is the 102-student island school: per-pupil costs have increased 36 percent in six years. While the services are appreciated, the high costs are of increasing concern to Islesboro residents. This is especially true for the very high proportion of retirees over 65 years of age living on fixed incomes, who account for 21 percent of the island's population, compared to 13 percent for the state.

PARADISE THREATENED

When the land rush in the 1980s came to Islesboro, the effect was to anneal the island community, both summer and year-round, into a united effort to chart a course for the island. "Subdivisions happened for the first time, and it was

unheard of," says Devens Hamlen, a third-generation Islesboro summer resident. "Over hundreds of years, Islesboro took care of itself." Suddenly, the balance was tipped by outsiders threatening to develop the island.

For the next 10 years, Islesboro took control of its destiny by undertaking a massive planning effort to steer growth on the island rather than let it fall prey to random subdivision. "The townspeople took action," says Hamlen. A detailed questionnaire went to 600 seasonal and year-round households, and received an unheard-of 80 percent response. "The uniform reaction between summer and winter residents favored some growth, but said that ecological values of Islesboro are paramount," says Hamlen. "They had to create a planning board, find building codes officers and people to look after things as they developed, and undertake subdivision and zoning ordinances for the first time. It was a big event." Hamlen and others formed the Islesboro Islands Trust, with the conscientious inclusion of equal numbers of summer and year-round residents on the board.

Hamlen alludes to support for school, affordable housing and land trust activities as proof of the longstanding trust between year-round and summer residents. Islesboro's blend of active retirees, summer people and year-round residents may seem an unlikely partnership, but their mutual trust appears to work. Islesboro seems content to remain on its present course for a long time to come. As if to secure it for the future, Islesboro's present character is etched in the Town's comprehensive plan, which states: "Islesboro is a small community of low-density single family homes on individually shaped lots along the town's narrow roads."

FROM DIFFERENT DIRECTIONS

All three of these Penobscot Bay communities have experienced major periods of transition, and all three adapted with ingenuity and resilience. In the case of Stonington, change appears imminent once again, but if history is a guide, her residents will make the best of it. If there is a common thread linking these Penobscot Bay communities together, it is the fact that their prosperity has depended on the abundance of natural resources at hand: in the case of Bangor and Stonington, it is from harvesting and adding value to trees, granite or fish; in the case of all three, the quality of life afforded by a healthy environment will be critical to their future. While all three arrived at that conclusion from different directions, they are united in their recognition of Penobscot Bay as a natural resource of exceptional quality and value.

Bob Moore *is a forester and freelance writer who lives in Freeport and contributes regularly to Island Institute publications. He is principal author of* State of the Bay.

DOWNTOWN ISLANDS

Boston Harbor's much-abused islands
may be getting a facelift

SCOTT ALLEN

Boston Light, Brewster Island   William F. Johnston

FOR YEARS, the old chimney stood over the skeletal frames of buildings and trash heaps, a reminder to passing boaters of the factory where the city once cooked and squeezed its garbage to recapture the valuable grease. Beneath the waves breaking on Spectacle Island came a faint tinkle from the broken glass among all the refuse that had grown up to 70 feet deep and actually increased the size of the island.

If islands could talk, what a grim story Spectacle would tell. Since Captain John Smith first sailed up Dorchester Bay in 1621, the island has been home to a smallpox hospital, illegal gambling halls, a rendering plant where horses became glue, and, until 1959, a dumping ground.

But, after lying fallow for three decades, Spectacle Island is about to be reborn. Engineers have completely covered the 97-acre island with fill from a downtown highway project, trapping Spectacle's past below and creating a vast beige mound on which landscapers plan to build a forested park complete with beaches, camp sites and walking trails by 1997.

The redemption of Spectacle Island is, in a way, the story of all the Boston Harbor islands, 30 gentle drumlins and rocky outcroppings that lie within one of America's busiest harbors. Like oxen on the farm, these have been working islands — the key to Boston's coastal defense, home to hospitals for the contagious and the dying, site of some of the most dramatic lighthouses in America, and generally a "back 40" where mainlanders hid their worst messes.

Aerial photograph courtesy of the Friends of the Boston Harbor Islands

Now the islands may find a new life as a playground and historic treasure for the three million urban residents who live within a few miles of them. Now that the $4.3-billion cleanup of "America's filthiest harbor" is making Boston Harbor safe for swimming and fishing again, U.S. Interior Secretary Bruce Babbitt wants to bring its islands into the national park system.

The National Park Service, which Babbitt controls, has proposed making the islands a National Recreation Area, creating an onshore visitors' center and dramatically expanding ferry service to at least 12 islands. From a resurgent osprey colony on Calf to the Civil War–era fort on Georges, a harbor islands national recreation area would provide a surprisingly peaceful oasis against the skyline of the financial district.

"The paradox is, for the last 100 years we used the islands as garbage dumps and as a back door to the city. Now we're going to make it the front door," said Babbitt on a visit to Boston last fall.

Babbitt became a fan of the harbor islands in 1993 when he visited Georges Island, dominated by the granite-walled Fort

Gallops Island, 1940

Warren where thousands of Confederate soldiers as well as the Confederate vice president, Alexander Stephens, were imprisoned. More than 50,000 people come by ferry to Georges each year, many of them armed with flashlights to tour the dungeons and tunnels inside the walls.

Standing at the gun emplacements where Union cannoneers once watched for rebel gunboats, visitors can watch the colorful spinnakers of sailboats glide past the nation's first lighthouse, Boston Light, on Little Brewster Island. In the foreground, the remains of a World War II gun battery still guard the beaches on Lovells Island. Only the slow clanging of a channel buoy breaks the quiet, even though jets take off from Logan International Airport less than five miles away.

Babbitt pronounced the islands a "national treasure" and announced a study of whether it would be feasible to bring at least some of them into the national park system. A draft version of the study calls for $29 million to $35 million in federal investment to create a recreation area similar to parks on the islands of San Francisco Bay and New York Harbor.

"I think it's Boston's turn," said Babbitt on a return visit to Boston last September, promising Congressional approval of the harbor islands plan by 1996.

Of course, Babbitt made his pledge before the 1994 elections swept the Democrats from power in Congress. The Republican takeover of both chambers is likely to make it harder to establish new national parks anywhere, especially in heavily Democratic Massachusetts. The islands' main Congressional patron, U.S. Representative Gerry Studds (D-Cohasset), not only lost his committee chairmanship in the power shuffle, but House Speaker Newt Gingrich also eliminated Studds's Merchant Marine and Fisheries Committee.

"It's really depressing," said Jodi Sugerman of Save the Harbor/Save the Bay, a Boston environmental group, "There's definitely impact on the Boston Harbor islands study. Not that it's impossible, but it'll be harder."

Even if the proposal for a national recreation area stalls, public interest in the islands is likely to remain high. Babbitt's proposal is part of a larger revival of Boston as a coastal city that has seen major expansions announced for the seaside New England Aquarium and Children's Museum as well as a new federal courthouse on the largest undeveloped waterfront lot in the city.

A return to the sea is inevitably a return to these islands, low-slung, forested presences that form the backdrop of almost every open water view from Boston. The federal courthouse, for instance, will include the harbor islands visitors' center as well as a ferry terminal for the vessels that will to transport passengers to the islands. And Massachusetts Governor William Weld has set aside $30 million in bond money to restore beaches around the harbor, including several on the islands.

Such enthusiasm for Boston Harbor would have been unthinkable in 1988 when President Bush tagged it "the dirtiest harbor in the country." At the time, he was right: pesticide residues and other toxic chemicals in the sediment were among the highest among all urban harbors, and 1.2 million homes in the metropolitan area flushed their toilets more or less directly into the harbor. As a result, the harbor's winter flounder were showing elevated tumor rates, and the beaches were chronically posted as unsafe.

Since then, however, the Massachusetts Water Resources Authority (MWRA) has built the second largest sewage treatment plant in the country, ending the illegal practice of discharging poorly treated sewage into the water. It hasn't been cheap: residents of 43 communities in the Boston area have invested more than $2 billion in the harbor cleanup so far, raising their sewer bills to among the highest in the country.

But the improvements in water quality have been dramatic. Rick Nolan, president of Boston Harbor Cruises, recalls the disgust he felt when he had to take passengers past a three-mile-long brown streak, a stinking plume of sewage flowing toward the Little Brewster lighthouse. These days, MWRA still discharges effluent into the water, but it is an unscented pale green. "You probably shouldn't, but sometimes [the water] looks so good you want to jump in," Nolan said.

Gallops Island today

In fact, state officials say the water *is* safe enough to swim in once more — health postings at harbor beaches have fallen by two-thirds since the mid 1980s, and beaches this summer are expected to be cleaner still because of the new treatment plant.

The cleaner water is bringing people back to the islands, said Ilyas Bhatti, commissioner of the Metropolitan District Commission, which got 100,000 visitors last year to the existing Boston Harbor Islands State Park, centered on Georges Island. "The future of the harbor islands has never looked brighter," said Bhatti.

At first blush, the Boston Harbor islands seem to have a lot in common with the islands off Portland in Casco Bay. Wedged between a city and the open ocean, they offer places utterly removed from the bustle and noise of urban life even though the sun sets over the office towers at night. And the history of both the Maine and Massachusetts islands, for better or worse, is intimately linked with the people onshore.

Despite the surface similarities, geography has dealt the islands sharply different hands. The islands of Boston Harbor are generally much closer to shore — Thompson Island in Boston Harbor can be reached simply by walking across the mussel beds exposed at low tide. As land-poor Boston expanded physically, the closest islands were simply filled in and made part of the mainland. Six former Boston Harbor islands are no more, including three that made way for Logan International Airport and two others for sewage treatment plants.

Second, the Boston Harbor islands are generally smaller than the islands of Casco Bay, and were never home to enough people to support the stores and services that communities on Long and Peaks Islands off Portland enjoy. There is only one permanent resident on Boston's islands — Ralph Kunkle, a teacher in the Outward Bound Program on Thompson Island. Another 42 families summer on Peddocks Island, but Massachusetts considers them "squatters" who must leave their cottages to the state when they die.

As a result, while the Casco Bay islands are vibrant private communities, the Boston Harbor islands are owned by a hodge-podge of government agencies. Each bears scars of centuries of human use dating back to when the Moswetuset Indians used them as convenient predator-free corn fields, but, today, most are devoid of human activity. Twelve are part of the state park, but only five can be reached by ferry (in summer only), and the majority are not maintained. Roofs on old barracks are collapsing and staghorn sumac is overgrowing pastures.

But this very neglect of the islands, especially after World War II, has left layers of unclaimed history to be discovered by a core of devoted island lovers and amateur historians. Edward Rowe Snow, the late nautical historian, called the Boston Harbor islands "one of the most delightful places in America." And the island stories he told offer a counterpoint to anyone whose idea of old Boston is the sophistication of Beacon Hill.

Snow particularly loved the legends; he singlehandedly popularized the curse of the Lady in Black. The woman, married to a Confederate lieutenant held at Fort Warren, tried to free her husband, but accidentally killed him when her gun exploded during the escape. Union troops, Snow said, hanged her as a spy dressed in mourning clothes. Over the years, Snow claims in his 1936 *The Islands of Boston Harbor*, sentries at the fort reported seeing her ghostly presence. One soldier was court-martialed for desertion despite his claim that he was "chased by the lady of the black robes."

Likewise, Snow delighted in the buccaneers who terrorized the harbor during the 18th century. He was one of the few visitors to Nix's Mate, the remains of an island all but washed away by the tides due to slate quarrying. Here, captured pirates were killed and hung in irons as a warning to other buccaneers.

Today, those with private boats can follow Snow's island-wandering to their heart's content, using his book, updated in 1971, as a reasonably accurate guide despite the years. The explorer will find empty beaches even on hot summer days and remnants of the past, from the colonial-era lighthouse to the Nike Missile sites that helped face down Nikita Krushchev during the Cuban Missile Crisis.

Two working lighthouses announce the entrance to Boston harbor and its islands. A 93-foot granite tower warns mariners of Graves Ledge, treacherous shoals that have claimed several ships, including the fishing boat MARY E. O'HARA that smashed into the rocks in a 1941 gale. "For hours the crewmen clung to masts swaying above the water," wrote Emily and David Kales in *All About the Boston Harbor Islands*, "until their hands froze and they succumbed to the icy seas." Only five of the 23 crew members survived.

More famous is the 1716-vintage Boston Light on Little Brewster Island, the prototypical New England lighthouse with its white tower and tidy keeper's cottage. The light, visible for 23 miles on a clear day, was so important to navigation that George Washington dispatched 300 troops to recapture it from the British during the American Revolution.

Today, Boston Light is the last manned lighthouse in the

United States, and the Coast Guard maintains a small museum at its base. Friends of the Boston Harbor Islands, a volunteer group that helps preserve the islands, periodically sponsors cookouts on the island.

Across the channel from Little Brewster sits 17-acre Calf Island, once the home of a colony of lobster fishermen and later the site of illegal boxing matches on summer Sundays. Here, actress Julia Arthur and her husband, Benjamin Cheney, built a 16-room mansion complete with theater at the turn of the century, part of the harbor islands' history as a retreat for the well-to-do. The mansion was destroyed by fire, but a stone chimney, bearing the husband's first two initials, "B.P.," remains.

Nineteenth-century graffiti in the stones on grassy Rainsford Island — "God care for us all for we are coming" — helps tell the story of patients at the Greek Revival quarantine hospital that once stood there, one of four island hospitals where the contagious either got well or died. Hundreds or even thousands of people died on Rainsford, the living patients separated from the graveyard by a 10-foot-high wall. One epitaph carved in neat serif letters shows a black sense of humor about the islanders' fate:

"Nearby these grey rocks
Enclosed in a box
Lies Hatter Cox
Who died of smallpox."

Castle Island

If Rainsford's mood is dark, Thompson Island, privately owned site of the Outward Bound Education Center, is its opposite, arguably the most beautiful of the harbor islands. A third of its 157 acres is salt marsh and tidal pond, while the rest of the island is covered with trees and wild flowers as well as a fine sand beach. At the education center, which includes housing for 150 students, inner-city youth learn about nature as well as leadership. "On Thompson Island," writes education center president Peter O. Willauer, "young people can use Outward Bound's proven experiential curriculum to set positive goals, develop personal strength, and grow through public service." The island has been the location of education programs for young people since 1833, when the Boston Farm School was founded to teach boys deemed to be at risk.

The dominant theme of these islands is, finally, the defense of the city of Boston. Though no shots have been fired in anger here since the British left town in 1776, soldiers guarded against enemy attack on at least 10 of the islands until fairly recently. Their leavings, from roofless pre–World War I barracks on Peddocks Island to spectacular Fort Warren, site of an annual Civil War battle re-enactment, are the most prominent pieces of history that the island explorer will find. All five of the state park islands that are accessible by ferry are home to significant military relics.

Snow, who devoted so much of his career to chronicling the islands, was at a loss to explain the lack of public interest in all this. "Strange how these islands, each an isolated pulpit, figured so prominently in our past, yet seem so destined for anonymity," he mused in 1971.

Today, as Interior Secretary Babbitt pushes to bring the islands into the national park system, island advocates are thankful for the years of obscurity. The alternative, until recently, would have been destructive proposals such as a system of bridges to connect key islands, a gambling casino for Peddocks

Island, and a sewage-burning plant for Long Island. All were rejected.

In fact, activists hope the Park Service can stop the one old-style island project that was not vetoed. The Boston police department has left Moon Island looking like the victim of a bad haircut, clearing all the vegetation on one side to make way for an expanded shooting range complete with a building where officers could practice "tactical assaults."

Marcie Tyre of the anti-shooting-range Seaside Alliance hopes that Moon Island will be taken over by the Park Service, putting an end to the police training area once and for all. "It's like when mom steps in and says, 'If you are going to pull the puppy apart, I'm going to take it,'" she said.

If Congress approves the National Recreation Area for the islands, however, the job of preserving the islands will only be starting. Even the best-preserved island, Georges, needs work — many chambers of Fort Warren are closed to the public because of decayed roofs and floors — while others such as Boston-owned Long Island are badly overgrown and full of crumbling seawalls and other hazards.

And the Park Service, no longer the affluent agency it once was, won't be able to do the job itself; it must pool resources with state and local agencies as well as private volunteer groups. As a result, the final shape of the recreation area will be determined in horse-trading among the various groups in the months to come.

Boston officials have already made it clear that, although they welcome the Park Service to the islands, they will not turn over city property — including their four islands — to them unless the federal government sweetens the pot. "I'm not willing to give anything up that the city owns without compensation," said Mayor Thomas Menino last fall.

Private groups, too, are staking out their positions for the upcoming debate. Boston's low-income and minority communities don't want to be left out during planning for access to the islands. None of the seven proposed ferry terminals would be in a minority neighborhood, mainly because waterfront neighborhoods in Boston are white.

"You have to wonder if it's a rational decision to take your family to a place they don't feel welcome," said Russ Lopez, director of the Environmental Diversity Forum, suggesting that minority families might avoid the island visitors' center proposed for South Boston, where racial tensions have flared.

Private businesses are also likely to want their cut of the action. Already, state officials say they have been approached about the possibility of bed and breakfasts, education programs and other amenities on the islands, currently home to a grand total of one snack bar. "Whether there are opportunities for public and private partnerships, if it is well thought out, it could be a benefit," said the Metropolitan District Commission's Bhatti.

But harbor island advocates say they would rather have debates over how best to create an island park system than go back to the bad old days when Spectacle Island was a city dump and many of the other islands weren't treated much better. As Suzanne Gall Marsh, founder of the Friends of the Boston Harbor Islands, put it, "The islands need help."

***Scott Allen** is a staff reporter for the* Boston Globe.

John, Ann, David, Karen and Gillian Gibson resettled in Cangaholt . Nutan (3)

The Irish SOLUTION

In County Clare, a resettlement project restores the rhythms of Ireland's rural "islands"

DEBORAH DuBRULE

ON THE COAST OF MAINE at the beginning of the 20th century, 300 islands supported year-round communities. Today, on the eve of the 21st century, that number has dwindled to 14. Two islands, Frenchboro and Isle au Haut (populations 40 and 65 respectively), have made concerted efforts to reverse the downward population spiral that threatens community survival. In the 1980s, with the help of a federal Community Block Development Grant and a tract of donated land, the Frenchboro Future Development Corporation built seven low-to-moderate-income homes to attract new families to the island. Following in Frenchboro's footsteps, in 1993 the Isle au Haut Community Development Corporation rolled out the welcome mats at three new affordable rental homes aimed at offering prospective newcomers a chance to try out island life and establish an economic footing before purchasing a town-owned lot and settling in for the long haul. The success of these programs still hangs very much in the balance.

While many of the difficulties of successful long-term resettlement might seem unique to the Maine coast (in particular, the challenges of adapting to isolated, inbred, staunchly conservative communities), a broader perspective suggests that the "core" issues — loneliness, boredom, finding meaningful employment, adjusting one's sense of scale — are in fact universal, or at least universally human. Journalist Deborah DuBrule spent several months in western Ireland researching resettlement efforts there, from which emerges the following fascinating sketch. While the details may be unique to the "Emerald Isle," overall, one can hear a familiar ring . . . and perhaps a few common strategies.

—Cynthia Bourgeault

Jim Connolly near his house at Loop Head

FOR OVER 20 YEARS, Irish sculptor Jim Connolly has walked along the same village road in west County Clare, imparting good wishes to the young who routinely leave to find work in Dublin or beyond, and attending the funerals of the old who remained behind, their windows perpetually darkened by emptiness.

"The population decline here in the west is catastrophic," says 59-year-old Connolly. "It's caused a lack of services and closed schools; shops and pubs have been boarded up; islands have been abandoned; the fishing villages are empty. My own village of Kilbaha is almost gone. . . . This is the scene throughout Ireland."

Dan O'Brien in his workshop

Whether it's an island off the coast of Maine or a remote rural village in the west of Ireland, each owes its uniqueness to the fact that only a few souls stubbornly endure its relative isolation, its intimate character and its fragile struggle with tradition and modernity. When even a single family is forced to leave, they remove a piece of the rhythm of everyday life. And all too easily, that rhythm can come to a halt altogether.

Ireland's population exceeded eight million when the potato blight struck in the 1840s. More than 150 years later, the population in the Irish Republic hasn't rebounded to even half that number. Emigration exerts a persistent drain on the population particularly in light of national unemployment, which reached a record 20 percent in 1994.

In the west, these tendencies are exacerbated. A declining fishing industry and a growing trend toward agribusiness rather than the traditional 30-acre family plots strengthen the inducement to seek one's fortune in the larger world. Migrating from green fields to seek jobs in Dublin, the young often discover limited or no job opportunities, the dole, and a waiting list of 26,000 people for government-owned "estate" housing.

"These are daft anomalies," insists Connolly. "The cities are overcrowded while there are thousands of empty houses in the west."

In February, 1990, Connolly emerged from his private life as a sculptor to propose on radio a scheme to connect the owners of abandoned houses in the west with weary city dwellers who wanted to escape the overcrowding, crime, alcoholism and drug abuse that typically surround them. His telephone hasn't stopped ringing.

Today, Connolly chairs the non-profit, non-sectarian organization called Rural Resettlement Ireland, Ltd. (RRI), which has relocated more than 140 families among 16 counties from Donegal to Kerry. Only nine families have returned to their former cities. RRI's waiting list exceeds 2,000.

"When my husband and I heard him, we thought it was too good to be true," recalls 42-year-old Breeda O'Brien. By the end of June, these native Dubliners and their eight children, now ages 5 to 19, found themselves embarking on a new life in the village of Coolmeen in west County Clare.

"When we lived in Dublin, we just couldn't bear to think about the future," said O'Brien. "People are everywhere. . . . We couldn't even feel safe leaving the kids alone."

The O'Briens lived in public housing, having been on the dole much of their married life. But rather than use their welfare check to pay rent on cramped housing in Dublin, they used their resources to rent a 100-year-old, three-bedroom stone house located just a few hundred yards from the Shannon estuary.

While all rental agreements are privately negotiated between immigrants and landlords, 20 of the 60 families who relocated to County Clare, including the O'Briens three years ago, have purchased their homes through government loans.

Their "village" consists of two houses (including theirs), a pub and a shop that also lodges the post office. "It's a hive of activity," laughs O'Brien, in her fast-clipped Dublin accent. "Everybody meets there to collect the dole and their messages."

Most of these new immigrants, as well as many western natives, subsist on public welfare, according to Connolly. In fact, social welfare, which includes unemployment compensation, outstrips the nation's debt payments, making it the largest budgetary government expenditure.

Far from ghettoizing the west as some had feared, the Dubliners are not only spending their dole checks on local goods and services (which cost more in the west), but are updating old homes, volunteering with child care and community groups, gaining election to school board positions, and helping to save local schools from closing.

"If we didn't have those five Dublin children [who relocated to Kilbaha], we'd be less one teacher at the local school," explains Connolly.

"We loved the idea of a country school," O'Brien recalls. "There were 1,000 children at the primary school in Dublin. Here, there are 38 on the roll with two teachers teaching four grades each. The quality of education is much better here."

> "They learn about things they've never been exposed to, like Irish dancing and raising farm animals and learning to play the tin whistle."

Isle au Haut
"I knew I didn't want to work in an office"

Like Jim Connolly in Kilbaha, Matthew Skolnikoff was himself an immigrant when he initiated a repopulation program through the Isle au Haut Community Development Corporation (ICDC), which he now directs. But seven miles from Maine's coast, "transplants" comprise the majority of the island's year-round population, which has grown from 35 to 65 since 1988. Seasonal residents swell the population to nearly 400 during the summer.

Skolnikoff had spent summers on the island during childhood and decided to return in 1988. "I had no idea what I'd do once I got here," recalls 30-year-old Skolnikoff. "I knew I didn't want to work in an office and live in a city."

With a background in community development, Skolnikoff offered his grant-writing skills to the town. A year later he helped form the ICDC to increase the island's population through a low-to-moderate-income housing project.

Researching Frenchboro's low-cost housing program before launching its own project, the ICDC completed three rental homes on two-acre lots in 1993.

After one and a half years in a rental home, Debra Schrader and her husband, Dave Hiltz, have purchased a two-acre lot from the town and will build their home this summer.

"Dave had been a sternman and decided he wanted to lobster fish full-time," says 27-year-old Debra Schrader, who manages the island store, which is owned by a group of islanders. "When you're a lobsterman, you can't just move somewhere, like Machias, and put down your traps or you'll be annihilated," Shrader explains.

"We couldn't afford to buy a home where we lived on Mount Desert Island. So when this came up," she recalls, "it was an opportunity to buy land at an affordable price, live in a small community that's not overrun by tourists, and allow Dave to fish from here because the established fishermen were accepting lobstermen to strengthen their association."

Despite the fact that two of the three newly settled families rely on fishing as their main source of income, Skolnikoff says that the ICDC also wanted to help diversify the local economy. "Not all of the islanders are employed in lobstering here, although that's the strongest sector of the economy," explains Skolnikoff. "Most people work at more than one job to survive here. Some have part-time jobs on the mainland."

In wrestling with the dilemma of how to attract new people without having jobs to offer them, the ICDC has established a low-interest loan program to enable islanders to expand, diversify or start a business on the island. "We're not planning to build any more homes at the moment," says Skolnikoff, "but we're hoping to buy more land for housing or for people looking to build who plan to stay here year-round."

Acadia National Park occupies half of the island's 5,500 acres and provides a few jobs. But mail boat service three times each day in summer ($18 round trip) and twice a day in winter ($10 round trip) allows far more freedom to islanders who wish to commute to the mainland for business, shopping or entertainment.

Marsha and Dave Quinby, who relocated from Peaks Island, have owned a marine biology business for 13 years, collecting specimens for scientific and school use and providing specialty seafood to food processors. When they moved to Isle au Haut, they hired another person to work with them, which, says Marsha Quinby, made them more appealing to the community in terms of acceptance into the program.

"We moved because Peaks had changed from a blue- to a white-collar community in 10 years," Quinby explains. "We figured we'd be zoned out in a matter of time, even though we were grandfathered. Besides," she yells above the din of a weekly playgroup that she and others formed at the community center, "I wanted to find more seclusion. . . . And when I find it," she laughs, "I'll let you know."

Because the Quinbys knew their move would be long-term, they negotiated the purchase of their home as a condition of relocation. Quinby wonders, if something happened to her husband, would she have to leave? "I don't know if I could physically make it here alone — if I could heft a propane tank, or cut wood. It's not like you can call someone and have a couple of cords delivered. You have to do a lot of things for yourself here."

— Deborah DuBrule

Not only are the children removed from a potentially dangerous urban environment, but, RRI's field worker, Sister Carmel Kehoe, says, "They learn about things they've never been exposed to, like Irish dancing and raising farm animals and learning to play the tin whistle." Kehoe helps relocated families with the sometimes overwhelming transition to rural life and connects them with friends or groups if problems with isolation or loneliness occur. (Many immigrants don't own cars.) Connolly, however, insists that Kehoe's job is "to work the miracles."

One miracle emanating from Connolly's scheme, and arousing interest from governments worldwide, lies in the fact that 15 percent of the immigrants have found employment or worked themselves off the dole, according to RRI administrator Paul Murphy who, with his wife and two children, relocated to Kilbaha five years ago.

"Those who participate in the scheme seem to find little niches in employment once they're here," said Murphy. "Many tried in Dublin and just got frustrated."

Of adaptation to rural life in the west, Murphy observes, "There are different forms of isolation. We didn't want the isolation of the city, living in

For mainlanders, no matter how rural, isolation is never so starkly irrevocable as it is on an island, in winter, storm lashing the coast, boat broke down, neighbors "ugly."

Frenchboro
"There were so many reasons we didn't want to leave, but . . ."

Faced with an empty savings account, a heap of unpaid bills, and a winter income totaling $33.33, says Elaine Beote, "We left the island not out of choice, but out of necessity. . . . Had we stayed, we would have had to go on welfare."

The Beotes moved to Frenchboro during the winter of 1988, along with five other families, as part of a low-cost housing program intended to strengthen the island's waning year-round population. Although one family with island ties remains in one of the six project homes, the Beotes are the last mainlanders from the original group of immigrants to retrace their seven-mile journey ashore. They follow a path worn by approximately a dozen families who have attempted resettlement over the last seven years and found themselves unprepared for the economic and social realities of island living.

"We fell in love with Frenchboro when we went for our interview in 1986 and we planned to spend the rest of our lives there," recalls Beote, who, with her husband, Stephen, waited two years for the completion of their three-bedroom house on an acre of land. "It was a chance for us to have our own home and we wanted to start our family there. It's beautiful. There's no crime or pollution — but there are no jobs either."

For some of the original immigrants who fished part-time, the move provided an opportunity to switch careers and fish full-time. In their early 30s then, Elaine was suffering from nursing burnout and Stephen was spending less time fishing and more time working as an electrician. "Stephen owned his own boat but he couldn't compete with the larger boats in Massachusetts fishing eight-trap trawls," explained Beote. "His boat was perfect for Maine where he could fish two-trap trawls and still remain competitive."

Matching income with expenses proved difficult from the start, according to Beote, who worked for a year as a teaching assistant at the island school and babysat the children of two of the island's school teachers.

"The fishing was terrible in winter," Beote said. "Stephen's boat wasn't equipped for scalloping, so he had to rely on being a sternman and doing electrical work to supplement our income. We went through our savings during the first year.

"Three years ago," she continued, "we thought we had finally gotten our feet under us when the boat engine had to be replaced. We just never caught up financially and last winter just did us in. The fishermen had hired permanent sternmen so Stephen went fishing as a substi-

Lunt Harbor, Frenchboro

shoe boxes next to so many other people. And I was in a dead-end situation. I was a bus driver and was always going to be a bus driver. I was writing, but wanted to devote more time to it." Murphy has just built a new home overlooking Kilbaha Bay, and his book describing his family's first year in the west will be published in September.

Like Murphy and others who grew disillusioned in the city, Breeda and Dan O'Brien have found their niche in a custom furniture business. "There's more potential to start a business here," O'Brien said. "In Dublin, there are too many people doing the same thing."

"We cast our net wide and asked for craftwork-type people to contact us [for resettlement]," explains Connolly. "This includes anybody who can make a living from their own enterprise, be it with their hands or an idea. I honestly believe that

Steve Beote, building his house on Frenchboro in 1988

tute sternman only four times and made $33.33 from January to April last year."

Not only was a shaky income from fishing disheartening, but newcomers also found themselves waging a similar battle with island expenses. To lessen their burden, the Frenchboro Future Development Corporation (FFDC), which organized and manages the program, reduced monthly rents over time from $475 per month to $350. Still, some families failed to balance earnings with expenses. When they left last summer, the Beotes had fallen six months behind in rent.

"Our electric bill was three times higher than it was on the mainland," Beote explains. "During the months when we used no heat, we paid at least $100 a month for electricity. Basic phone charges ran at least double the mainland rates."

Transportation to the mainland for basic goods and services was a challenge as well. The ferry visits Frenchboro one day each week and doesn't return until the following day. Round-trip fare with car: $32. Islanders with no place to stay on the mainland pay an additional $45 for a motel — expending more than $75 before they've bought a loaf of bread. "Shopping was a major event," laughs Beote, "but after the first year, it got easier."

Anxiety about the future of their three-year-old son, Louis, also guided the

"[The islanders] had no concept of the changes we had to make to try to fit in."

Beotes' decision to return ashore. "There were so many reasons we didn't want to leave, but I had some concerns about the education children get at the island school," said Beote, who served on the school board for several years.

Frenchboro's teenagers move ashore when they enter high school, unlike those on nearby Swan's Island, where students are ferried daily to and from the mainland. "Even if children get an education [on Frenchboro]," insists Beote, "they don't learn socialization because the class size is so small. When they're forced off the island to attend high school, they have a terrible time fitting in and some don't adjust at all."

Newcomers to the island enter not only a closely enmeshed community, but one rooted in a strong family network. Less than 40 people comprise Frenchboro's year-round population and many natives are related, sharing a long history with the island. "Sometimes, it was difficult to find someone to talk to," Beote remembers.

While some of the settlers admitted to Beote that they had no intention of remaining on the island beyond five years, she says she saw other families leave the island after taking sides in various disputes or by disturbing the status quo. Recalls Beote, "We never took a side and we got along with everybody. But, especially as a newcomer, once you take a side, you've got a good chance of becoming unpopular with the islanders."

Beote says that as an advisory board member, she recommended to the FFDC that prospective immigrants be given an

accurate picture of daily island life, rather than stressing the positive aspects to the near-exclusion of the negative. Although the board agreed with her, said Beote, "They never really changed their approach in courting people. I think they'd have a better chance of keeping families on the island by giving them a clearer idea of how hard it is, the level of isolation, the expense, and even what the community expects of them."

Islanders said non-involvement with the community led to discontent among the newcomers, especially the women. Conversely, Beote and others found islanders somewhat aloof. "When we moved there, no one came by the house to welcome us or to let us know that they were there if we needed some help or whatever," said Beote. "If islanders made more of an effort to make people feel welcome and feel that they were part of the community, it'd make one helluva difference. I'm not a very forward person and I never felt comfortable enough to go through the village and introduce myself or, later, to visit people without being invited. . . .

"[The islanders] are so accustomed to their way of life — it's a hard and isolated life, but it's uncomplicated and so different from where we all came from — that they had no concept of the changes we had to make to try to fit in. I think more people might have been encouraged to stay if they had shown some empathy for the adjustment we all had to make to adapt to everyday life there."

Both Stephen and Elaine Beote had been elected to paid town jobs shortly before leaving the island and Stephen's name appears four times in the 1993 town report in various non-paying municipal jobs and committees.

"We were happy on Frenchboro. I miss my house and the quiet and the friends we made," says Beote. "This was the first year that I felt somewhat accepted by the community."

— Deborah DuBrule

Steve Farrell, newly resettled in West Clare, works at Spear Vegetable Garden.

"There are different forms of isolation. We didn't want the isolation of the city, living in shoe boxes next to so many other people."

these are almost the only people who eventually can survive in a rural area where there aren't large factories or employment. . . . But there are opportunities for people to develop here and it was almost inevitable that we must start something that would try and assist them at that level then, through craft development."

In cooperation with the vocational education board in County Clare, Rural Resettlement Crafts (RRC) was established three years ago to help locals and settlers alike in pursuing craftswork businesses. This offshoot organization has also helped launch crafts holidays for tourists, as well as county-wide craft fairs.

"But if we didn't have paid staff," says Connolly, "we couldn't run any of this."

During the first two years, Connolly operated with a few private donations and out of his own pocket, even borrowing a horse trailer to help a couple of Dublin families make a move which, in itself, is economically prohibitive for most living on minimum incomes. The group operates largely from private donations, although it receives a government grant which meets administrative costs for six full-time staff. Most recently, Connolly has received a commitment from the Irish government to match any funds he can raise in the United States.

New York attorney Hugh Finnegan has established tax-exempt charitable status for "RRI, USA," primarily in response to Irish-American interest in Connolly's project and its success. "The donations so far are pretty modest," said Finnegan. "What we're really looking for is a benefactor to remove the headache Jim Connolly's had in running the organization on a hand-to-mouth basis."

Connolly's future plans involve establishment of a fund through which RRI would buy and restore houses and either rent or sell to settlers. He wants Catholic parishes to help in locating one affordable home per year for the next five years to rent to future settlers. With seasonal residents driving up the price of homes and property, locating affordable, livable rental housing in the west has become a problem.

Connolly's newest challenge lies 30 miles from the coast on the island of Inishmaan, one of the three Aran Islands where Irish is spoken as a first language. The islanders plan to bolster their sagging population with 10 new houses within the next two years. Five of the homes will be rented to islanders who live on the island or wish to return from the mainland or abroad, and five families on RRI's waiting list will relocate from Dublin.

RRI and a group of islanders will conduct classes with the five families to help prepare them for island life. The Dubliners are being offered fishing opportunities and it is hoped that some of them will open their new homes to tourists by offering bed and breakfast during the summer as many islanders do during the tourist season.

As Maine islanders who live on Frenchboro and Isle au Haut insist, it takes a special person to live on an island. For mainlanders, no matter how rural, isolation is never so starkly irrevocable as it is on an island, in winter, storm lashing the coast, boat broke down, neighbors "ugly." Seven years into their resettlement experiment, citizens of Frenchboro seem to be resigning themselves to viewing the new recruits as temporary reinforcements rather than permanent new additions. Islander Sandra Lunt echoed the sentiments of many in saying, "I'm just grateful for whatever time we get from them — even if they can only give us a few years — because they help keep the community going." But as the resettlement efforts on both sides of the Atlantic clearly demonstrate, imagination and persistence can accomplish surprising things.

Proprietors, Roosevelts, and Scoundrels

FOR TWO CENTURIES, CAMPOBELLO'S STORY HAS BEEN ONE OF FOREIGN CONTROL

JANICE HARVEY

WITH ITS POPULATION of about 1,200 people, Campobello is the second largest of four settled islands in the outer Bay of Fundy. It separates Grand Manan Channel from Passamaquoddy Bay, a unique and biologically prolific body of water once called "pes-te-no-ka-tek" (meaning "the place where pollock abound") by the Indians living there. Like the other Fundy islands, its economy and culture are dominated by the sea.

Despite early efforts at farming, brick-making, logging and other manufacturing, Campobello islanders have consistently shown themselves to be best suited to earning their livelihoods from the sea around them. There are about 260 licensed fishermen on Campobello, engaged in a year-round fishery for herring, lobster, scallops and sea urchins. The once bountiful groundfishery is virtually gone, but salmon aquaculture has developed and today one local salmon farmer and processor is the single largest employer on the island.

Franklin D. Roosevelt sailed Campobello's waters with his family.

The vast majority of the island's land base, however, has long been outside the control of the fishing families living there. Over 225 years and three distinct eras, outside control has been dominated by one or another "Campobello Company," with each new landowner, in a somewhat perverse way, borrowing the name and the legacy of its predecessors.

The era of the most recent Campobello Company came to an end in the summer of

Admiral William Fitzwilliam Owen, the third Principal Proprietary, arrived on Campobello in September, 1835.

1994, when one-third of Campobello's land mass was turned over to a Maine real estate broker for sale on the open market. Six months later, an American bought the property, promising to take islanders' wishes into account as he planned its future.

Further complicating the story this time was the third Campobello Company's association with James McDougal, the Arkansas speculator who had also participated in a controversial and politically charged scheme called Whitewater, and whose list of investors in that scheme included the President of the United States.

To islanders the story of the third Campobello Company was familiar: a land speculator's bubble had burst, leaving locals with difficult choices and largely at the mercy of an outside owner with stated good intentions.

After a century of being tenants on their own island, and a second century of absentee landlords and developers controlling up to two-thirds of the land, Campobello's traditional "live and let live" way of life is clearly under serious strain. Once divided between pro-development and anti-development camps, Campobello Islanders are today divided on a strategy for asserting some control over their own future.

To know Campobello and its people, we must know the story of the three Campobello Companies and how each — for a time — came to dominate life on the island.

Traditionally, weir fishing was a mainstay of Campobello's economy.

THE FIRST CAMPOBELLO COMPANY

On August 28, 1769, a small group of men gathered in a coffee house in Warrington, a town between Liverpool and Manchester in the north of England, to discuss a potential investment in British North America. At the head of the table was Captain William Owen, a Welsh navy officer recently discharged as British and French hostilities eased. Two years earlier Owen, in lieu of a military pension, had been named Principal Proprietary of the Great Outer Island of Passamaquoddy by Lord William Campbell, then Governor of Nova Scotia, a region that also included present-day New Brunswick.

The first Campobello Company was formed with 12 investors or subscribers plus Owen as the landowner. On June 3, 1770, Owen landed on the Great Outer Island, named it Campo Bello (for his benefactor Campbell and for its beauty), and began the settlement of New Warrington. With him were 38 Lancashire settlers, most of whom were poor indentured servants who had left wives and children behind, 15 crew members and Captain Plato Denny, a company shareholder and master of the company ship SNOW OWEN, aboard which they sailed.

Thus commenced Campobello's era as a colony. Owen claimed ownership over the entire island of 13,000 acres. In addition, he was assigned the powers of magistrate over all of Sudbury County (now New Brunswick), making him judge and jury as well as landlord.

In 1771, Captain Owen returned to England when another war between England and France seemed imminent, offering an opportunity for military men such as himself. Captain Denny was left in charge. The population was now 73, half English and half New Englanders. While the latter consisted of families, all but four of the English were men indentured to the company and had left families in England. One year later, according to some accounts, the English mutinied. Captain Denny was forced to set sail for England, with 27 of the original Lancashire settlers aboard. They never made it: the ship went down off Newfoundland.

Only nine of the original Lancashire settlers remained, seven of whom soon moved on to greener mainland pastures. Apart from Andrew Lloyd (whose grandson was William Lloyd Garrison, editor of abolitionist newspaper *The Liberator*) and two agents of the Campobello Company, the rest of the population was made up of New Englanders. In the face of growing hostilities between England and the 13 Colonies and the uncooperative attitudes of the remaining settlers, the Campobello Company investors voted to dissolve in 1775, leaving Owen and his heirs in sole possession of the island.

Captain Owen was killed in India in 1778. Nine years later, in 1787, the captain's nephew, 33-year-old Squire David Owen, educated at Trinity College, arrived on Campobello to claim his inheritance as second Principal Proprietary. Islanders, by that time, assumed the title had been forfeited. According to author Alden Nowlan in his book, *Campobello, The Outer Island*, the residents "were infuriated, understandably enough, by the irony of David Owen claiming that his family had complied with the conditions of the grant 'by cultivating and improvement as to have freedom from forfeiture' when it was they — the people whom [David Owen] treated as squatters and trespassers — who had done all the cultivating and improving."

Squire Owen's reputation was infamous: it was said of him that "his meanness was as low as his pride was great" and that he was a man of "deep intrigue and inveterate prejudices." Still, he was successful in ousting all the speculators who had appeared in the interim years.

The Squire loosened his grip on the island somewhat when in 1820 he began to sell parcels to those islanders fortunate enough to scrape together a little cash. This marked the beginning of the village of Welshpool, nestled around Friar's Bay. After a feisty and cantankerous reign of 42 years, the second Principal Proprietary died in December, 1829. His body was shipped back to England for burial, perhaps to punctuate his feeling of having been exiled to this remote place. In his will, he left Campobello to his cousin, the son of Captain Owen.

Admiral William Fitzwilliam Owen, the third Principal Proprietary, arrived on

Today, salmon pens have largely replaced weirs.

Campobello in September, 1835. Four hundred people lived there then, to whom Admiral Owen added his wife, two daughters, two shiploads of settlers, cattle and supplies. He was 61 and had completed a long career in the navy and as a cartographer.

He took to the island and his duties with gusto, calling himself the "Quoddy Hermit" and, in contrast to his predecessors, engendering much admiration and respect within the island community. As much as possible, he lived the life of landed gentry. Tyn-y-Coed, his grand house built from wood imported from England and using the frame of the Squire's house, stands today on its original site, Deer Point. (The house was moved to make way for a resort hotel in the 1880s, but the hotel was subsequently torn down and the house moved back into place.)

Admiral Owen controlled virtually all aspects of islanders' lives. He financed the beginning of the weir fishery in the Bay of Fundy in 1840; 10 years later there were 21 weirs off Campobello, employing (including boats engaged in the fishery) 252 men and boys out of a total population of 865. He established his own bank and currency with which he paid those who performed public service such as road-building. He conducted church services and, in 1855, built St. Anne's Anglican Church, in which services are still held. The needlepoint chancel carpet and altar vestments made by his wife and daughters still grace the beautiful chapel.

Admiral Owen controlled virtually all aspects of islanders' lives.

When Admiral Owen died in Saint John in 1857 his body was brought back to Campobello. He was buried there amidst local expressions of grief and much ceremony. He was succeeded by his son-in-law, Captain John James Robinson-Owen, the fourth Principal Proprietary of the Outer Island, who followed more in Squire Owen's unsympathetic footsteps than those of the benevolent Admiral. These were hard times. The combination of a free trade treaty with the U.S. and the depression of the 1870s hit people hard and Captain Robinson-Owen was known to evict the "old and infirm" for non-payment of rent.

In the midst of the depression, Captain Robinson-Owen initiated efforts to sell the island. He died in 1874, his efforts unsuccessful. His widow, Cornelia, the last of the Owen line on Campobello, assumed responsibility for their holdings. In 1881, 111 years after her grandfather had set up the original Campobello Company to develop his land grant, she found a buyer: the second Campobello

Company, formed by a group of investors out of Boston. Headed by Alexander S. Porter, they set about to make Campobello a summer resort for the rich.

THE SECOND CAMPOBELLO COMPANY

American capital, American enterprise and American culture have laid hold of the little island of Campobello, and with a quickness savouring the days of Aladdin have transformed the old possessions of Admiral Owen into the most charming watering-place in the world. (Saint John Daily Sun, July, 1882).

So began a new era in Campobello history. Over the next few years the new Campobello Company built three resort hotels to house American visitors who traveled by private rail car and steamship from Boston to Eastport every summer. It was to the Tyn-y-Coed Hotel, named after Squire Owen's house, that James and Sara Delano Roosevelt and one-year-old Franklin came in 1883. So taken were the Roosevelts by the island that two years later, their own 15-room summer cottage on 10 acres overlooking Friar's Bay was ready for occupancy. (The James Roosevelt cottage has been torn down. Franklin and Eleanor Roosevelt purchased their cottage from the estate of Mrs. Hartman Kuhn for $5,000.) Other wealthy Americans who built "cottages," either as investors in the Campobello Company or as purchasers of land from the company, were Samuel Wells, Dr.

A unique new seat in the New Brunswick Legislature

ERIC ALLABY

In the next general provincial election, New Brunswick will adopt special recognition of islands. A unique constituency has been created, including only islands within its bounds.

The islands off the coast of Charlotte County — Campobello, Deer Island and Grand Manan — share much in their heritage, having similar economies, values and interests, and all have problems of geographic isolation.

While the concept of distinct representation for the islands may appear to be new, it is, in fact, an idea almost as old as settlement in the area. The first island representative, from Campobello, was elected in 1795. In 1822, a petition was

drafted to the King of England praying that Deer Island, Campobello and Grand Manan be made a separate county, but nothing came of it. Several islanders sought nomination and election as Charlotte County members of the Legislature in the late 19th century but met with limited success.

In 1935, a tradition was established that the slate of four candidates put forward to represent each political party in the County of Charlotte would have on it one islander to represent the interests of islanders in the provincial capital.

In 1974, the Province was divided into single-member constituencies. The islands of Fundy were separated and attached to mainland parts of Charlotte County, and the concept of "island member" faded from the County experience as the interests of the islands became more assimilated with the mainland.

As an islander from Grand Manan, I was elected in 1987, and re-elected in 1991, and when the re-drawing of elec-

toral boundaries was undertaken, I made strong representation for the recognition of the distinctness of islands and their special needs and circumstances. The Electoral Boundaries Commission was sympathetic to the arguments put forward on behalf of the islands.

Thus the Province of New Brunswick will be recognizing officially the distinct nature of islands. The House of Assembly was reduced from 58 seats to 54 seats plus a unique 55th seat for the Fundy Isles, a seat with one-third the number of voters of other constituencies, but justified on the basis of the very difficult geography of islands that must be overcome in serving the people. This is a significant development for the voice of islands within representative government, and affirms what everyone who reads *Island Journal* already knows: islands are special.

A Liberal, Eric Allaby plans to stand for election to the new Fundy Isles seat at the next opportunity.

Campobello's economy and culture are dominated by the sea.

At the Campobello museum

Russell Sturgis, Alexander Porter, Gorham Hubbard and Mrs. Hartman Kuhn of Boston; Travers Cochrane of Philadelphia; Alfred Pell of New York; and L. L. Prince of St. Louis.

Unlike the 100-odd years under the rule of the Owens, in this period local people went about their business largely untouched by the summer resort. The biggest impact was felt by the village of Welshpool, since that was where the hotels and summer homes were located. Many people in Welshpool were hired to service the summer people in the hotels, in their homes, and on the water. But far from being aloof from the community, according to Welshpool resident Joan Lord, "the summer people blended in; they were part of the island. They went to church services and fairs, people here babysat their children and worked for them. The coming of the summer people each year marked the beginning of the season for everyone." Joan Lord's father, Murray Johnston, ran the mailboat between Campobello and Eastport. He used to carry Eleanor Roosevelt's newspaper columns for the *New York Times* across to Eastport for posting. As a young girl when FDR died, Joan's first thought was, "What will they do with the dog?"

The wealthy Americans, especially the Roosevelts, brought prestige and attention to Campobello, a change from the notoriety it enjoyed as the Owen fiefdom. However, the prestige has overshadowed the island itself. From the time of the second Campobello Company, the island's story outside this context becomes lost as the Roosevelt mystique takes over.

The boom time of Campobello tourism only lasted about 25 years. By 1910 the

Today, Campobello's traditional "live and let live" way of life is under serious strain.

hotels had run their course and were torn down. What remained were the grand family cottages; over time these too would decline in use. Franklin Roosevelt, for example, only returned to Campobello for three brief visits after contracting polio there in 1921 (even though Eleanor returned each summer with the children). After his death, the cottage was sold to Armand, Harry and Victor Hammer of New York.

The second Campobello Company must have bought at least 60 percent of the land mass of the island, or 7,800 acres, from the Owens. Islanders now own about 40 percent of the island acreage; it

is not clear whether any of this was purchased from the second Campobello Company or whether it had all been acquired from the Owens before this time. Nor is it clear when the second Campobello Company disposed of those assets remaining after the summer home market dried up. In any event, the hiatus between this and the third Campobello Company did not free up the land to island ownership. Instead, a new era began that saw both private and public ownership of the company lands.

By the mid 1940s, Dead River, a forestry and railroad concern based in Maine, was the single largest landowner on

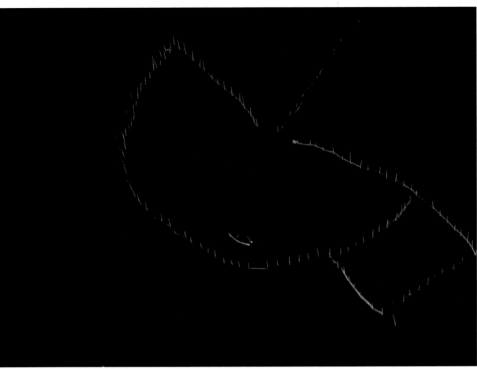

Many herring weirs like the one above have disappeared.

Campobello, probably having bought out the Campobello Company lands. Their holdings were extensive, including the rugged, inaccessible lands on the "back of the island" where cliffs face the Grand Manan Channel. For a time the company carried out logging operations. Once the economic expediency of this changed, Dead River became a passive absentee landlord of whom the islanders were largely unaware.

In 1964, government established its presence with the opening of Roosevelt Campobello International Park, made possible by the donation of the Roosevelt Cottage by Armand Hammer. Since then four other cottages have been acquired by the Park. The Hubbard and Prince cottages flank the Roosevelt cottage; on the other side of the road are the Wells-Shober and Johnson cottages. These acquisitions plus Hammer's gift and some donations of land by Dead River, now total 2,800 acres, or over 21 percent of the island.

Campobello's experience with the park has been mixed. Administered by an international commission whose members are appointed by the President's and Prime Minister's offices in Washington and Ottawa, islanders have had virtually no voice in park management, with one exception. Commissioners are high-profile political appointees, including a former Lieutenant-Governor of New Brunswick, New Brunswick real estate millionaire Mitchell Franklin, Dead River chairman Curtis Hutchins, Senator Edmund Muskie and Franklin Roosevelt Jr. The exception to this tradition was Murray Johnston, the former mailboat

The wealthy Americans, especially the Roosevelts, brought prestige and attention to Campobello.

operator, who was appointed in 1964 to the first commission for one year. No one from the island has served since.

Many islanders still see the Roosevelt Campobello International Park as land apart from the community, in spite of the 130,000 to 140,000 visitors it brings to the island each year. According to Dale Calder, a fifth-generation native, the Park has done little for the overall development of Campobello. "It promotes itself, not Campobello," says Calder. From his vantage point at the Customs House on the Campobello end of the Roosevelt International Bridge linking the island with the U.S. mainland at Lubec, Maine, Calder sees the ebb and flow of visitors to the park, which sits just beyond the bridge.

"Ninety percent of the people who come to the Park see the film at the reception center, the Roosevelt Cottage, two rooms of another cottage, and they're out in 30 minutes. Bus tours never spend more than an hour on Campobello," says Calder. "A few new tours take people to lunch at the Lupine Lodge or Friar's Bay Restaurant just beyond the Park, but that's as far as they go. I never see a bus

beyond those two restaurants in Welshpool."

In the 1970s, island park land was expanded once again. On 1,048 acres adjacent to the Roosevelt International Park, the provincial government established the Herring Cove Provincial Park, managed by the Department of Natural Resources in Fredericton. Together, these two parks total 3,848 acres, or nearly 30 percent of the island.

As a kid, Dale Calder resented the Roosevelt Park because of the land it controlled. The provincial park added fuel to the fire. The third Campobello Company changed all that. Today he is relieved those parks are there.

THE THIRD CAMPOBELLO COMPANY

In 1983, James McDougal, then President of Madison Financial Corporation of Little Rock, Arkansas, lifelong activist in the Democratic Party, friend of Bill Clinton and a self-avowed Roosevelt devotee, saw an ad in the *Wall Street Journal*. Dead River was selling its holdings, roughly 4,000 acres, on Campobello Island. Together with Christopher Wade, owner of Ozark Realty Company of Flippin, Arkansas, McDougal began to act out his dream of recreating the Roosevelt era on Campobello, 1980s style. The two were partners in another real estate deal, Whitewater Development Corporation, encompassing 230 acres in Arkansas.

They formed yet another Campobello Company, a subsidiary of Madison Guarantee Savings and Loan. Madison Financial Corporation, also an affiliate of the savings and loan, was managing partner. After negotiations, the partners bought 3,900 acres for $825,000, or about $211 per acre. Half of the price was picked up by the Madison Financial Corp. The other half was covered by Wade, with a loan from the savings and loan. In essence, the Madison Guarantee Savings and Loan was in for 100 percent. (Shortly after, Wade was bought out by Jerry Jones, owner of the Dallas Cowboys, and Sheffield Nelson, Republican candidate for governor against Bill Clinton in 1990. The Clintons were not investors in the Campobello Company.)

Curtis Hutchins, president of Dead River and park commissioner, reportedly first offered the acreage for sale to the Roosevelt Campobello International Park. Walter Hunt, a Dead River executive and financial consultant to the park, said that the commissioners did not want the land because it didn't "enhance the existing park and the Roosevelt Cottage itself." Before it was sold, 20 adjacent acres were donated to the park.

(continued on page 92)

WITNESS TO THE DEEP

DAVID CONOVER

ONE DAY, over a decade after lift-off, the Voyager robotic spacecraft reached a point on its outward journey where visual contact with the earth was about to be lost. For no scientific reason, astronomers turned its cameras back and focused them towards home. There in the distance was a tiny warbling speck of pale blue light. Another few hundred miles of travel and the blue light disappeared.

Experiencing the threshold between a known light and the deep has been no less mysterious and no less compelling for generations of mariners and lighthouse keepers. At this threshold, a lighthouse guides the voyager with a tangible comfort that no radar, no radio, no GPS, no outer space navigational system will ever replace. The connection is primordial, residue of a nomadic, campfire-centered past. In the darkness, actual visual contact with a known light tells us *where* we are. In the darker darkness, it tells us *that* we are.

Five years ago, a Norwegian friend and I were groping our way ashore in a small sailboat, having been dismasted towards the end of an arduous transatlantic passage from Europe. As navigator, I hadn't been able to get a celestial sight in nine days, but rough calculations and our electronic instruments put us 30 miles off the Cape Race Light of Newfoundland, an island landfall light that was the first sight of North America for millions of immigrants. We were closing in on the rocky cliffs. Night approached. We wanted to see land, to see a light, to know where we stood. Suddenly, our electronics told us we were in Winnipeg, thousands of miles away.

Illustrations from a special book by Siri Beckman, reviewed on page 95 of this *Island Journal*.

Searching for the light that night was one of the many times I have understood the significance of a light for a mariner. If you have not been to sea at night, imagine this. You're confused, possibly lost. Darkness distorts the strength of the wind on your face and the size of the waves beneath your hull, making everything far away seem ever so close. "Where is that light?" you ask as you strain to see. Your look into the dark during these moments is absolutely sincere, absolutely focused, like the reaching of the shipwrecked for that first piece of floating debris, because finding the light may mean your salvation.

Some years later, I had the opportunity to meet the man who had been the keeper of the Cape Race Light that night, safely perched high on the cliff. Fred Osborne had been a keeper for over 30 years, following the course of his father and grandfather. Cape Race was his last assignment, one of the few remaining manned stations on the entire eastern seaboard of North America. He didn't have much to do, except keep the place spotlessly clean and occasionally wander

up the winding steps of the 96-foot tower. As a hobby, Fred kept a ham radio watch with the call sign VO1JO. The keeper at Cape Race, he told me, was the first land station to receive the SOS of the sinking TITANIC.

Back then, mariners depended on more than the beacon being there. Like the pale blue light of distant island earth, all lights were lived in, kept, not remotely controlled from afar. A tower was built under the light and houses were built next to towers. A keeper was always nearby. The light was a home, an extension of domestic architecture, another odd-shaped room in a simple house where brass was polished, bread baked, cows milked and a watch kept. Unlike navigation lights today, the lighthouse station was designed not only to be seen, but also to see. For the keeper, the light tower was like a giant optical instrument, a watchtower during the day, a magnificent lens and articulated light at night. Eyes and observation mattered in this place, a visual place. This fact often goes unappreciated because most people know light stations from afar, looking *at* the light from a boat at sea or a car on shore rather than *with* it like Fred Osborne.

In Maine, my family have been seasonal residents of a former lighthouse for over 15 years. Our caretaking responsibilities do not include the fixed green light itself, only cosmetic work on the tower. The Coast Guard stops by every six months for the light, which is still active and automated. Consequently, I've always felt a visitor to the tower, apart from it and its original purpose. I've often wondered how the task of tending the light affected the lives of the keepers, what they thought about, imagined. I've read first-person accounts of keepers' lives, looked through the extensive amount of lighthouse literature and images available in the coastal bookstores and museums, but still find myself returning to the structure itself, viewed up close.

I imagine a keeper's trip into the tower late one night sometime in the 1800s, perhaps to fill or pressurize the kerosene lamp. This task had to be done every four to six hours, around the clock. The heavy door is unbolted and swings open with a creak. The tower is dark inside, still and

attic-like, with a smell of machinery oil and smoke. Sounds bounce off the circular walls and echoes layer on echoes as one ascends the curved stairs. At a landing, a crack of light from the ceiling trapdoor shines on a ladder. When the trapdoor is opened, light floods downward. The keeper eventually reaches the top room, checks the flame, then adjusts the wall vents to match the wind change and keep the correct draft. The lens and the blue glass around the lamp need dusting, but that is nothing compared to the outside windows covered with moths and bugs attracted to the biggest night light around.

There is a small door to the catwalk outside, where the wind and the sound of the surf can be heard below. Outside, a few steps away, the keeper could look back. The light is green, a color that results from the yellow beam of a lamp passing through blue glass. Turning towards the darkness, the light appears reddish as the cones and rods in the eyes struggle to compensate. The green beam hangs in the faint night mist, focused by the Fresnel lens to a 15-degree arc that covers all the water except for the surf below. A light would only reveal the danger of that place.

The mind wanders for a moment, following the beam projected out. Down in the distant darkness, a passing sail of a coastal schooner provides a tiny white screen for the light to play out its colored ID. Faint voices carry with the wind. The keeper's eye sees shadows — never noticed those before — black arms radiating out, one arm for each of the catwalk's railings and each of the window supports for the glass. Walking around the tower catwalk, the keeper sees the white house next door is also bathed in green. I wonder if the keeper's hands would ever make a shadow rabbit on its wall before heading down to ring the bell. That rabbit would be two stories high.

Keepers of the 1800s were communicators in a different age, before the telegraph, the wireless, the telephone, and the age of information. Back then, communication was tied to the limits of the human body and the pace and direction

of its movements from place to place. If you wanted attention you shouted, blew a horn or waved a flag. Letters were hand-delivered, carried by someone who walked or rode a horse or a train. News was understood in context, usually local and relevant. Hardly ever was it trivial. People paid attention to it, because it was accompanied by other people. Every message had a messenger. A lighthouse keeper was an

extraordinary messenger with a singular goal: keep the light lit. To this end, each keeper was dedicated.

Along with the light stations, the keepers have attracted a good deal of attention from those romantics in love with the sea. Solitude, adventure and a unique positioning at the shoreline have everything to do with this. The light stations, whether they be coastal on a mainland peninsula, among the islands, or further out still on a rock, were always the gateway through which dreams of escape to the open sea could pass. As the energy of these dreams passed on to the keepers themselves, the question arises: Of what must those gatekeepers have been made? How did they remain calm in the storm, prepared for being cut off from supplies, with the imperative of keeping the light burning organizing their life? Eternal vigilance is the price of safe navigation, and the keepers paid the price.

Born in an age when lights were powered by the flames of a whale oil lamp and ships were powered by the wind, these aids to navigation marked a coastal waterway that was the only Interstate of the day. By the late 1970s, however, the situation in almost all the Maine stations had changed. Keepers packed their trunks with tools, paint and polish and walked down to the boats, leaving their towers and houses behind like outgrown shells. These shells had capacity, but no longer any purpose. The age of sail had passed. Most coastal traffic had moved ashore. Lights became powered by a generator or by the mainland electrical grid. Initially, the keeper's houses were boarded up and minimally maintained by Coast Guard commanders with a strong nostalgic attachment to the stations. Gradually, a few became used as research stations, museums or parks.

Many years into the future, an archaeologist uncovers a primitive structure along a shoreside cliff. A signaling cairn of some sort, a few thousand years after the Druids and Stonehenge. A Promethean attempt to bring the fire of the stars to earth. A time when the ocean was important and central to people's lives. What will that archaeologist understand then, and what understanding will he have lost? Attention is then turned skyward, to remote travel to distant planets, where stars are once again navigational aids. Looking back, the blue light remains. The magic of the light station is understood, perhaps, forever.

David Conover is a documentary film producer in Camden.

Christopher Ayres

Filament after filament

*Chebeague artist
Shirley Burgess sews
a web of connections*

KATE KENNEDY

Facing page: It took less than five months to create this queen-size quilt with panel pictures of 15 different lighthouses, all hand-stitched and hand-quilted. "If Shirley gets an idea about something, it's as good as done," says her daughter-in-law.

OVER THE MANTELPIECE in Shirley Burgess's living room on Chebeague Island, Casco Bay, hangs one of her own large oil paintings. Before you've even taken a seat, it invites you to walk down the weed-choked cart path from the Higgins place, an old salt-water farm, to Ed Jenks's house. From the present to the past. When Shirley took the photos for this painting, the path was still there, just as she remembered it from girlhood in the days Ed Jenks and George Higgins went back and forth for a game of cards. "Ed was somebody we cared about," says Shirley. "I look at that path, and I think about the two old fellows who were friends." The other living-room paintings speak to that same attachment: one depicts her father's fish house, seen from the outside; one its interior. For Shirley, there's a story at every turn of the path, in every tool on the workbench.

Shirley Burgess was born on Chebeague in 1918 and graduated as valedictorian of her class from the island high school in 1936. In another time, she might have attended college, but she doesn't dwell on what might have been. Shirley is too busy with what is and with creating what hasn't had a chance to be yet. Still, she urges her own daughter, Sharon Bowman, to go on past a master's degree. A teacher and writer, Sharon now lives and works on the mainland but has spent most of her life on Chebeague and still keeps a camp there. "My mother is a visionary," she says, "in the sense of the creative process. She believes in a continual state of becoming, and she lives by the creative principle. She's always encouraging people to realize more than they think they can realize."

Shirley is an artist. It's a family talent, she says, running through the Rosses, as well as many other island families. Her grandmother made and sold hooked rugs, her mother braided rugs and did all sorts of handwork from tatting to crochet. Shirley's sister, Frances Todd, does fine upholstery. This artistic ability has traveled from Shirley to her children and grandchildren, a strong cord binding one generation to another. Her younger son, David, makes and sells models of boats and carved whales, mounted on driftwood, as well as mobiles of sailing craft, correctly proportioned and rigged.

Since early girlhood, Shirley has drawn and painted, carved sea birds, sewed, made quilts. "When I was 10 or 12, I used to paint shells and have a stand — Chebeague souvenirs. All over the island the kids made little stands like mine. It set off an epidemic. A boy named Willie Eves, the pianist, would come running over to my house and he'd look at what I was painting and say, 'Thanks for the idea.' One day I was so mad, I chased him up over the hill and I beat him up and tore his necktie in two. At the time I was a big girl, very athletic. Afterwards, his parents came over to my house. 'Look what Shirley has done to poor Willie,' they said. 'He's two years older,' said my parents. 'If he can't manage that girl. . . . ' But all he seemed to paint was blueberries. He was no big threat."

"Our house smelled of turpentine," Sharon Bowman recalls. "You'd reach for a glass out of the cupboard and there'd be a ring of paint around it, and it might taste of turpentine for a day or two. If she wasn't carving, she was painting. If she wasn't painting, she was quilting."

Sharon's brothers, Ernest and David, both of Chebeague, agree. "I used to come in and there on a cookie sheet would be little coat pins she was making, pins with sets of earrings — mallards and pintail ducks," Ernie, a fisherman, remembers. A whole generation of Chebeaguers, now in their 40s and 50s, still talk about the great times they had when Shirley was involved with Scouting. "She made all kinds of art projects for the Cub Scouts to do — totem poles. They loved it," says Ernie. "She'd whip up these little kits with blocks of wood of different shapes and sizes. They'd all make wooden trucks. She could do things in a few minutes that would take other people weeks."

To make ends meet, Shirley picked crabs, sold her handiwork through the Maine Arts and Crafts Guild, carved game birds for a hunter's resort in Delaware, worked as a hairdresser. There were some hard years. Then, starting the in early 1960s, she became the Chebeague postmaster (she doesn't like "postmistress"), a job she held for 22 years. When Shirley remodeled her house in 1970, she attached a post office, which she leased to the Postal Service. In 1984, she retired to devote herself to her art work and to the organizations and causes in which she believes. People still ebb and flow through the door from Shirley's living room into the post office. Her flower beds and hanging pots of

bright red tuberous begonias still decorate the little post office parking area. She stays connected. Her son David's cabin is close by. Ernie and his wife, Sue, live just down the road.

Everyone agrees Shirley's a dynamo, a whirlwind, a phenomenon. But what's most inspiring is that she fulfills herself as an artist while at the same time helping countless worthy groups. And it's all

Shirley Burgess doesn't dwell on what might have been. She is too busy with what is and with creating what hasn't had a chance to be yet.

Of her most recent quilt, designed and made by hand to benefit the Island Institute's Maine Lights Program, Shirley says, "I wanted to make something that would count."

of a piece. In recent years she's organized quilt projects for the Chebeague Island Hall Community Center (of which her great-grandfather, Edward Ross, was founder), the Chebeague Library Fund, and the Cumberland Mainland and Islands Trust, which helped raise enough money to buy Stockman Island, a bird nesting ground, and to protect it from development. Not only have the quilts raised money, but they've brought before the public's eye issues that are important to Shirley. She's political and savvy enough to know that beautiful quilts attract attention. Of all her mother's quilts, the one Sharon admires the most has panels picturing Stockman Island. "Shirley hadn't been to Stockman in about 44 years, but she retained her memory of the beauty and captured it in cloth," says Sharon.

Once people see her devotion and caring for something, Shirley believes, they'll want to help. So far, it's worked. She's passionate about preserving the environment, historic sites, institutions that serve people well. "Chebeague is a caring community," she says. "There's a style of island living for older people, and I'm in it. The secret is to get involved in organizational structures, and then people look out for you, outside the structure. I cannot give a lot of money to different groups. I can't find many people who are willing to pay me thousands of dollars to make quilts for them. But I can contribute my talents."

Early last summer, Shirley was excited when she heard about the plan for the U.S. Coast Guard to transfer 33 of

Maine's 70-odd lighthouses to the Island Institute, which in turn would pass them on to towns and preservation-minded groups as well as federal and state agencies. The idea stirred her. Of her most recent quilt, designed and made by hand to benefit the Island Institute's Maine Lights Program, Shirley says, "I wanted to make something that would count." No one sought her out for this mission; she volunteered. New navigation technology and automation of the lights have rendered light stations almost obsolete, endangering their survival. In recent years, the Coast Guard has been under increasing pressure to cut costs by disposing of light towers, keepers' houses and grounds, sometimes whole islands. Luckily, there are enough people who love lighthouses for their history, architecture, and aesthetic and symbolic importance that the Institute was able to find owners eager to take care of all 33, and to ensure public access.

Her daughter-in-law, Sue Burgess, puts it this way: "If Shirley gets an idea about something, it's as good as done." It took less than five months to create this queen-size quilt with panel pictures of 15 different lighthouses, all hand-stitched and hand-quilted.

When pressed about exactly how many hours this took, Shirley shrugs. "You don't count time. You just take joy in it, creating and doing something right, from scratch. I work when the spirit moves. They don't turn out as well when you're not enthused. It's not the 'Now Generation.' What fun is there in how many you can turn out? It's a sickness of the times we live in. It works against the craftsmanship," she insists. By all accounts, the spirit moves plenty.

Chebeague itself has no lighthouses, and Shirley's passion for the Maine Lights Program seems an anomaly until she explains. "Chebeague has a lot of history connecting it to lighthouses — so many people whose ancestors not only carried the granite blocks that made the lighthouses in their stone sloops, but built the lighthouses and maintained them, even worked as keepers. So many involved, all over the island."

Joan Robinson has a photo album full of postcards — over 100 — that her grandfather sent to her grandmother when he was maintaining lighthouses. Ray Hamilton's grandfather hauled granite, Ray Newcomb's grandfather, too. Dick Bowen's great-great-grandfather Hugh and his great-grandfather Henry sailed to lighthouses with mail and supplies, made repairs when buildings were damaged by storms.

Bill Ross and Elsie Hamilton's grandfather Joseph Upton was a keeper at Matinicus, Isle of Shoals, and Two Lights in Cape Elizabeth. "I used to loved to go up in the lighthouse," Elsie recalls of childhood visits, "though I wasn't allowed up very often. I liked the winding stairs, looking out and seeing boats, and at Two Lights you could look right straight out and there was Halfway Rock, which isn't how it looks from Chebeague."

In fact, Joseph Upton, while head keeper at Two Lights, died on the job in January, 1934, just two years short of retirement. A terrible winter storm kept knocking the electricity out. Twice he climbed up into the light, holding a lantern. The second time he was gone so long that Elsie's grandmother began to worry. She too climbed up the winding iron stairs. There he was, collapsed on one of the landings where he'd fallen, his head bleeding from a gash.

As important as lighthouses were to the economic well-being of so many Chebeaguers, for Shirley there's an even more compelling connection. "People don't realize how many lives were saved up and down the Maine Coast by lighthouses before they had radar," she says , "the wives and children who'd be affected, not to mention the fishermen themselves. And how many of us on Chebeague wouldn't be here today if it weren't for the lights."

Shirley's father was a fisherman. So is one of her sons, and her ex-husband. In January, 1975, both sons, together with Cecil Amos Doughty, were long-line trawling on Platt's Bank, about four and a half hours from Halfway Rock. Suddenly, a screeching gale of 70 or 80 knots blew out of the southwest. From there, it took them 11 and a half hours to reach land, at Boothbay. "Everybody on Chebeague knew about it because we thought we'd lost them," Shirley says, "Not having at that time the electronic devices to navigate by, only compass, the lights at Seguin and the Cuckolds guided them to safety."

Chebeaguers knew most of the lighthouses in Maine; they fished up and down the entire coast, in and out of every cove, sardining. It's not just the light they recognized — each one distinct from every other according to its color and signal — but also its sound, whether horn, bell or siren. Most photographs of lighthouses we see are taken from adjacent points of land, not from the perspective of those at sea, notes Ernie Burgess. "You don't realize what it was like for fishermen to travel by dead reckoning with sight and sound. You steer by compass, figure wind and tide. You figure your vessel speed and time, then you depend on seeing the light. We used to stop and listen and get a bearing on a fog horn. Years ago, it was a perilous business. All you had was a compass and sounding lead, your eyes and ears. Lighthouses look awful, awful good when you're not sure where you're going, especially in a snowstorm at night."

There is snow in Shirley's lighthouse quilt, and there's night and day, sunrise and sunset, winter, summer, storm and calm. What's most striking at first is color — vibrant color. Then movement. The 15 lighthouses pictured, all part of the Maine Lights Program, are stable beacons, but the appliquéed and embroidered land and seascapes around them swirl with motion. Waves crash against Goose Rocks, and water boils with foam at Marshall Point. In most of the quilt panels, clouds roll down the sky. At Rockland Breakwater, the green, light-dappled ocean is washed with pink and lavender and with the paler green of cloud reflections. "She's painting with fabric," Sue Burgess says. "And this is a real quilt with stitching all the way through all the layers, which gives it its depth and texture."

Shirley worked with photographs of each lighthouse. Then she drafted the picture in black and white, and from that made a template, used as a pattern. "You start in with the background and fill in toward the foreground, like oil painting," Shirley explains. "I tried to be exact with the buildings — the proportions, the placement of doors and windows, the color of roofs, the number of red stripes on the West Quoddy Head tower. I also want the rocks and ledges to be the same. But I got kind of fanciful with the backgrounds to create interest in the seasons and different times of day."

Like most quilters, Shirley collects fabric. She subscribes to four quilting magazines and routinely sends away for samples. Friends who travel bring back interesting textures and designs. In her bedroom are two trunk-size boxes of fabric, one trunk downstairs as well as numerous bags stashed here and there. For the lighthouse quilt, she used all designer-cotton material, some hand-painted: "top-grade stuff." Shirley also likes the battings you can buy now and special quilting material showing the seasons of the year.

"I choose my colors first," she says. "I like planning it and getting most enthused about it, hauling out all my fabric and making a big pile of everything I'll use and maybe changing it 50 times before I get it right. The blending and the shading is so difficult with fabric."

To create the illusion of round light towers, Shirley shaded some with dye, some she embroidered, for others she used two different fabrics. The water-based dyes are painted onto fabric then set with a hot iron, which makes them permanent. The only place she painted after she'd put the panels together was inside the windows.

After completing the individual panels, Shirley laid them all out on her bed and arranged them in a way that pleased her, she explains. Spring Point Ledge in South Portland is the center panel. "It's something I know, and to me it's one of the best pictures." After organizing the panels, Shirley quilted them together by hand. She enjoyed this, too, what to some is tedious work. To Shirley it's simply part of the process, part of the pleasure.

When she finished, Shirley didn't donate the quilt to the Island Institute. Instead, explains Donna Damon, Chebeague historian extraordinaire, she gave it to the Chebeague Historical Society to give to the Island Institute. "Shirley believes in the interconnectedness of all organizations," Damon says. "When people first come to Chebeague, they have trouble understanding why one non-profit organization would donate to another, but it's part of the island culture. All groups are related, one group of people to another." And so the logo patch of the Chebeague Historical Society appears in one corner of the Lighthouse Quilt, and Shirley's embroidered name in the other.

The quilt made to benefit the new Chebeague library was, in fact, another project sponsored by the Chebeague Historical Society. Nearly 30 island women helped create the panels. Shirley coordinated the effort, made some panels herself and did the final quilting. Proceeds from the raffle went to the library fund. The sale of postcards with a photograph of the quilt benefited the Historical Society. Both organizations shared profits from posters of the quilt, raising a total of $6,500 for the new library, $4,000 for the Historical Society.

What next? Already Shirley's involved, as financial officer, in a fundraising campaign to save the Chebeague United Methodist Church. Already she's planning another quilt to benefit the church, the only one left on the island. And after that — who knows? But something important, something of value. They are messengers, these quilts, calling us to preserve and admire the natural world, to restore endangered traces of our history and to keep the bonds of community strong. Like the lighthouses, they remind us to take good care.

The poet Walt Whitman describes his own work this way:

The soul, reaching, throwing out for love,
As the spider, from some little promontory,
throwing out filament after filament, tirelessly
out of itself that one at least may catch and
form a link, a bridge, a connection . . . .

For Shirley Burgess, these filaments catch and hold, each one.

A summer resident of Chebeague, **Kate Kennedy** *teaches creative writing at Portland High School.*

Galen (left) and Ted Turner of Swan's Island

THE PAST IN BITS AND PIECES

On Swan's Island, two brothers have decided to protect the island's maritime history. On an island, that means protecting just about everything.

ANDREW WEEGAR

In their home/shop/dooryard on Swan's Island, Galen and Ted Turner have slowly, hands-on, over the past decade accumulated an impressive variety of artifacts and old photographs. The materials preserve a fascinating era of Swan's Island maritime history that might otherwise have passed unnoticed.

In the process, the Turner brothers have made some fascinating discoveries that challenge traditional assumptions of maritime historians, particularly with regard to the Swan's Islanders' contributions as boatbuilders and innovators. The Turners' work is known to the Smithsonian Institution and to curators at the Bath and Penobscot Maritime Museums, where it has been judged to be of "museum quality." And a museum is what the Turner brothers would like to build — right there on Swan's Island.

But of course, museums on most islands and in coastal communities are founded, organized, funded and maintained by summer people, or year-round residents "from away" who can "talk the talk" and find the grants. High-school educated, self-taught, and with the intimately practical perspective of native-born islanders, the Turner brothers have so far failed to attract the recognition and funding their work so eminently deserves. Is there something wrong with this picture?

OVER THE PAST decade, Ted and Galen Turner, two brothers from Swan's Island, have made an effort to find and protect everything they could about the island's maritime history.

Most of what the brothers have saved is stored in the yard around their shop and at Galen's house, both of which back up on an abandoned quarry in the island town of Minturn. As the owner of a considerable pile of material myself, I considered what I saw impressive. Outdoors, beyond the usual old cars and lumber, the flotsam of island history seems to be made up of miscellaneous pieces of unidentifiable rusting metal. On closer inspection these turn out to be winches and engine parts from the old quarry, several other antique engines retrieved from the bottom of the local harbor, plus other items the origins of which are more obscure.

In the house, things are in better shape, but hardly more orderly. A Glenwood cookstove in the kitchen is buried under a pile of old ledger books and binders full of photographs. There are store account books, catalogues. Where do you begin with a pile like this? "I'm not really sure," Galen says. "It's kind of like trying to tell you the history of the United States in a few minutes."

Telling the story of how they began this, like the effort itself, takes both of the brothers. Galen does most of the talking, with Ted either nodding in agreement, adding an occasional pithy comment ("He's dead," "flu got 'em") or correcting a name or a detail.

Galen: "We've been at this for quite a few years."

Ted: "Ten."

"When you live on an island," says Galen, "and you know you're going to be stuck there for the rest of your life, sooner or later boredom sets in and you decide you might as well have a look around. And then you figure you've got to have to have some kind of mental activity to keep from going crazy."

Over the years, the Turners have tried several projects to keep from going crazy. "We got into Indian relics. Spearheads. Then we got into old bottles."

As good a starting point as any for understanding the Turners' endeavors

came more than a decade ago, when a dump truck pulled into the yard of their Minturn house and deposited the burnt-out shell of what had been a lobsterboat.

The Turners decided to resurrect it, a decision that attracted considerable attention, especially from other boat-builders. Galen recalls getting plenty of free advice: "Local builders would come by and say, 'It can't be done. Even if you wanted to fix it, you don't even have the plans.'"

The Turners were undaunted. Typically, they decided to teach themselves enough to save the boat. First, Galen recalls, they read a book on boatbuilding, then they measured stations of

Galen and Ted Turner, with part of their collection

what was left, attaching longitudinal wooden ribbands to hold the stations plumb in the boat. Luck was with the brothers when a summer resident, the president of a fiberglass company, noticed their efforts, and gave them some chopped glass remnants and some resin. They applied hardware cloth, bonded it over with fiberglass and faired the finished hull. The boat was essentially saved.

The Turners' new boat had, by any standards, a troubled past, and the brothers were mindful of that when they renamed her. Before the fire that sent her to the Turners' shop, she'd been run into and swamped. Even before that, says Galen, "she had fallen off the truck on the way to her launching."

After the fire, the boat's original owner put her engine in another boat. "That boat sank." Her radar went to still another boat. "That boat went ashore and smashed up." The Turners gave her a new name: SUPERSTITION. "We've run her since, without a bit of trouble."

The story of how the Turners set about saving the SUPERSTITION demonstrates the remarkable determination the brothers bring to their

endeavors. When they wanted to explore an old wreck in the harbor, for instance, they simply bought some scuba equipment and started using it.

Restoring the SUPERSTITION, however, also got the Turners thinking about boats, and about the boatbuilding history of the island. This increased when Galen took a course in photography through the island's adult education program. "We borrowed every old photograph we could find and took a picture of it," says Galen.

"After a while, there's no sense taking pictures of the family and all of that," says Galen. "A relative had a picture of his grandfather. I thought that would be neat to have, so I borrowed it." Another islander had old negatives, but no pictures. Galen borrowed the negatives and made prints. "I started seeing all of these boats," he said.

Although the Turners had heard stories of boatbuilders on Swan's Island, they knew little about them. They read what they could and set about looking. They discovered that finding physical evidence of boats and boat shops was something else again, in some ways more difficult than finding Indian relics.

Few records survived of working boats on the island. "A lot of the clipper ships were saved, because that was what was interesting," says Galen. "But the day-to-day boats, that stuff was lost. There's no record of the fellow that built a lobsterboat in his backyard." The owner of a clipper might have a painting done of the boat, the owner of a mackerel boat would not: not only would that have been an unaffordable luxury, the idea of it would likely have been incomprehensible. To fishermen, boats were simple utilitarian craft. "Even today, most fishermen don't know much about boats except you grab ahold of the wheel," Galen says. "If you're making money, you don't hold on to a boat. You get rid of it and get a new one. A lot of that stuff didn't stay around too long."

Some information remained where the Turners could find it, mostly in the lofts and attics of other island residents. "We've come across, I'm going to say, 60 or 70 half models," says Galen, referring to the scale models the builders used to fair their designs. Even this number is insignificant given the number of boats that were built on the island. One builder alone, Llewellyn Joyce, built 101 boats. "When he died, there were only two half models."

"Many of them were destroyed," says Galen. "Others were given to the people the boat was built for." Some were sold off the island as decorative art, others were likely burned in the shop stove in winter.

The Turners' search for boat history took them all over the island. Ted runs a gas route, giving him access to everyone on the island, summer person and resident, and he spread the word of the brothers' interest. Galen searched out the tax records, and the two asked islanders for photographs, half models they could measure and rebuild, anything at all to do with boats. "It wasn't always easy," Galen says. "You're talking family heirlooms, and you say, Can I borrow them for awhile?"

Probably one of the most remarkable stories uncovered by the Turners is that of the NOVELTY, a mackerel vessel built and operated by an islander named Hanson Joyce. For 40 years beginning about 1820, Swan's Island had a productive cod fishery. In 1819, the U.S. Congress passed a law providing bounties to the owner of any boat that fished for cod at least four months out of the year. For the next four decades, until the cod laws were repealed in 1866, most of the island's fishermen went to sea for cod. With the repeal of the bounty laws, they switched to mackerel, fishing for them with hand lines from Chebaco boats and pinkies. In 1871, an islander named Freeman Gott began to fish for mackerel with a purse seine, and for the next 20 years, Swan's Island had either the largest or second largest mackerel fleet in the country.

During most of those years, Hanson Joyce was the most productive fisherman in the New England fleet. Joyce stayed on top through innovation that at times was almost herculean in scale. In 1885, when the mackerel fleet consisted of elegant sailing schooners, Joyce decided sailing was fine, as long as there was wind. Since there sometimes wasn't, Joyce designed and built a steam vessel he named the NOVELTY. At the time, it was one of the largest steam vessels in the world.

Joyce operated the NOVELTY for several years. Around 1890, however, the mackerel disappeared, and the fishery

never recovered. The New England Fish Company hired Joyce to build a halibut steamer, which Joyce sailed around Cape Horn to San Francisco, where he built two more.

The NOVELTY was sold to the Cuban government, and was rammed by a gunboat in Puerto Rico during the Spanish American War.

There is a remarkable pride in acquaintance on Swan's Island, as perhaps there would be in most communi-

SUPERSTITION, *before and after*

ties its size. The closeness of the island's community was almost the first thing Ted Turner spoke of when he met me at the dock. "Out here, everybody knows everybody." No sooner had he said that than a beat-up van drove off the ferry. Ted waved, and the driver waved back, hesitant. Ted frowned. "Well, not everybody. We're getting a lot of urchin divers out here. We've got Russians, we've got Vietnamese, who knows what else."

The island is changing. On an island where everybody knows everybody, what is as surprising is what they don't know. "Nobody around here has ever even heard of the NOVELTY," says Ted. When the Turners looked for information on the ship, they found it in a surprising place: the Smithsonian Institution in Washington, D.C. A half

model went to the Smithsonian as part of the collection assembled by noted nautical historian Howard Chappelle. Galen ordered the plans and began to build a scale model. Right away, however, he noticed a few mistakes. Launching records for the NOVELTY showed she was 150 feet long. The plans were for a boat of 112 feet.

The boat plans had been scaled from a photograph. The Turners found more when they mentioned the NOVELTY to an islander named Bradley Joyce. He *had* heard of it, "in fact, he had a picture," says Galen. Whereas the Smithsonian's photograph shows a slanting view of the ship, this picture showed her in full profile, and revealed more mistakes in the Smithsonian's plans. "The plans showed straight masts," says Galen. "The masts had an obvious rake."

Galen finished his model of the NOVELTY, which now sits on his kitchen counter. Have the Turners notified the Smithsonian of the mistakes in the museum's plans? "No," says Galen. "There isn't time. That information is safe. There's other stuff out here that's disappearing every day."

The Turners have made other discoveries. The accepted word on lobstering boats, for instance, is that they came from New Hampshire. The Turners question that. "There was a fleet of schooners out here that numbered about 130," says Galen. "If something can be built locally then nine times out of 10 it will be. If they needed to look at a boat, they didn't need to go to New Hampshire to do it."

As the Turners look for other material, their approach has been to cast a very wide net. "We have used what I call the scatter-gun approach," says Galen. "What should you save and what shouldn't you? If it's marine-related, you save it." Ted agrees: "Our approach is 'Drag it home, because you ain't gonna see it again.'"

Much of their collection includes other marine- and fishing- related gear. "We've got stacks of ledgers from some of the fishing companies," says Galen. "Everything and anything we could find that was related to fishing." There is a set of numbers fishermen displayed to patrols during the Second World War, a wall of half models, a sign from an old mail boat. "I traded a bottle of Jack Daniels for that," says Ted.

A motorboat company on Swan's Island near the turn of the century outfitted its boats with inboard one-lungers. "You're talking about early motors," says Galen. "One-lungers, make-and-break. They were cast, then polished by a machine shop."

In time, many of these motors were used as moorings. "They came along during the two World Wars and collected what was left for scrap," says Ted. The Turners went out into the harbor after as many as they could pull up: in their yard, three motors sit in a lonesome pile. "You pull 'em out, they look like a million bucks," says Ted. "All smooth and gray." Overnight, they rust.

The brothers set about finding one in better shape. "We couldn't find one on the island, we had to trade with someone on the mainland." They traded one for another until they had an old Lathrop from Johnson Island.

Not knowing anything about one-lungers, they typically decided they would fix it. Much of it was missing, and the piston was seized. "We tried heating it," says Galen. "We tried oiling it, we tried a car jack underneath it to lift it." When that worked, they had another problem: it was now stuck in the raised position, and they had to use the jack to force it down. Finally, it was freed. Hundreds of hours later, it sits smooth and black on the Turners' floor. Galen turns it over, and it gives a steady hissing noise and rhythmic snort.

The brothers collected other bits of fishing history. Next to the restored one-lung motor is a tank standing nearly six feet tall, iron and glass, used to separate cod-liver oil. A steam coil in the bottom cooked the livers until they separated, then water was introduced into the tank, and the oil rose to the top, where it ran out another pipe. The cooker also served a second career as a mooring; the brothers rescued it in a rowboat, using a rope looped into a windlass. "It was quite an engineering feat to do it," says Galen.

"When we brought it up to the shop," says Ted, "a guy who lives right down there" — he motions toward the waterfront — "he came running out. He remembered what it was for."

That kind of knowledge made the Turners' work easier, but also gave it another edge. "It became an imperative to get it done now," says Galen, "while

there were still people who remembered what this stuff was, what the boats were and what they were about." Often, even this was not enough: some of the changes that have occurred within recent memory are difficult to document. Most of the island fishermen used wooden traps well into the 1960s, but the brothers hunted the island before they could find one. The Swan's Island traps are unique: rather than steambent bows, island trapmakers bent green spruce boughs into an arc, then mortised them into two spruce stretchers. The traps were woven with steamtarred cotton. Galen found a roll.

The efforts have gone beyond preserving the past. Galen has traveled

Galen Turner and his model of NOVELTY

around the island, recording some of the fishermen's current activities. Swan's Island lobstermen store lobsters in pens in the harbor called "lobster cars" — layers of lobsters are put into the cars in the fall when the prices are low, separated by dividers called "flakes." "The harbor's full of 'em," says Ted. How many layers are there in a car? The brothers don't know, but they consult the drawing.

"For the Turner brothers to do what they've done — actually canvass the island, find all the old photographs, and copy the negatives — is remarkable," says Nathan Lipford, the librarian at the Maine Maritime Museum in Bath. "I've never heard of anyone doing anything like that. Sometimes a scholar might, or a researcher might try to come in from the outside and do that, but they're much less likely to be successful than an islander."

The question is where the Turners go from here. There is a clear sense the two would like to see their material go together in a museum. "We're right next door to one of the most popular national parks in the country," says Galen. "If I was going out west, I'd want to see a museum about cowboys."

"We want to tie this all together with some of the things that are hard to

find," says Galen. "But it's hard. We do this on our own, with no funding." The Bangor Public Library has a copy of an early history of Lincoln County, which used to contain Swan's Island. Galen has wanted to read it, he says, but "by the time you get down there, and get a ferry fare, and you stay overnight, well, that blows that idea."

At times, the lack of funding has led to the loss of irreplaceable opportunities. "There was a fisherman who had lived here," says Ted. "He moved to Portland. He was 102. I wanted to get down and see him, but he died." Ted says the same thing may happen with a neighbor on the island. "He was a 'ripper,'" Ted says, a man whose job it was to cut a fish so it would lie flat when it was packed in salt. "He's one of the last people who knows how to make all of the cuts on a fish. He worked for Johnson on Swan's Island, then he went to work in Bass Harbor. On the mainland, Ted says, "That fellow didn't like the way he made his cuts, so they fired him. I want to get a video of it, but I don't have a camera."

While Nathan Lipford says that the work the Turners do is the sort of work that would interest a number of private foundations, he questions whether the Turners would be successful if they applied for grants to fund their work. "They might have trouble applying to a normal funding agency," he says. While there is little doubt the Turners are doing museum-quality work, Lipford says the Turners "don't talk the talk."

"They don't know the humanities jargon they'd need to write a grant proposal," Lipford says, adding that Galen has carved half models as good as any he has seen. Turner himself is more modest. "I can carve something that looks halfway decent."

"The Turners might do better with a private donation, or with an individual," says Lipford.

So far, that individual is elusive. The Turners press on. Galen mentions tiring of the whole pursuit one minute, then mentions a number of half models that need carving, and a winch he has heard about hanging in a fisherman's shop. "I need to get down there and measure it," he says. "I guess you never tire of the chase."

Ted mentions a cannon rusting away on a summer person's lawn. "I haven't been able to get it from him yet," he says. "I will."

Andrew Weegar writes for Maine Times.

Iris at Sea, *oil on panel, 1994*   *Jamie Wyeth*

SOUTHERN

CHRISTOPHER CROSMAN

SOUTHERN ISLAND and its lighthouse, signalling the entrance to Tenants Harbor, have been the subject of dozens of remarkable paintings over a period of the last 15 years by Andrew Wyeth and his son Jamie. Not much more than a dot on many nautical charts, Southern Island is approximately 22 acres of grass, rock and a few windswept spruce. It is only a few minutes from Tenants Harbor by boat, but the lighthouse itself, located on the opposite side of the island, looks out to a sweeping view of the open Atlantic with only the faintest trace of Matinicus Island in the far distance. The fetch, they say, is Spain.

The lighthouse, dating to 1857, was extinguished in 1934 and restored in the late 1970s by Betsy James Wyeth. It became Andrew and Betsy's private retreat until 1990, when they moved to another island farther out to sea off Port Clyde. Eventually, Jamie Wyeth moved his principal studio and residence to Southern Island from Monhegan, in part to find more privacy for his work.

Kitchen Porch,
watercolor, 1980

Andrew Wyeth

While the Wyeths, father and son, rarely stray far from home for their subject matter, their Southern Island paintings are exceptional for their sharp, intense and prolonged focus on this small patch of land. Just as the prisms of a lighthouse lens strengthen and concentrate a beam of light, so, too, the paintings by both artists illuminate this island with flashing clarity and emotional precision. With its connotations of searching and illumination, Southern Island lighthouse is a potent metaphor for art of both Wyeths.

Comparisons between Andrew and Jamie Wyeth's paintings on Southern Island would appear inevitable and obvious. However, as conveyed through their antipodean visions, Southern somehow becomes very different, infinitely mysterious and variable, as if seen through the opposite end of the same telescope.

Binoculars,
watercolor, 1981

Andrew Wyeth

The earliest Southern Island paintings by Andrew Wyeth, such as *Kitchen Porch* and *Binoculars*, appear to be nearly reverse views from virtually the same vantage point outside, as if the artist suddenly wheeled 180 degrees to capture both what was before and behind him. One view is looking back into the house and the other out towards the sea (the same bench appears in both). In neither work is there any real indication of the lighthouse. But the subject of both paintings seems to be light itself, steady and nearly blinding in *Kitchen Porch* and about to be extinguished in *Binoculars*, with

ISLAND LIGHT

This special folio addition to Island Journal *is made possible by a generous grant from the Charles Engelhard Foundation.*

an approaching squall at sea. The binoculars clearly refer to the traditional purpose of the lightkeeper, long absent, but whose ghost lingers in this silent place. Light and dark, near and far, solitude and presence, past and present, timelessness and change, the trope of the artist watching and seeing — all are contained in these spare, concentrated watercolors.

Another sea-change, this one social and historical, is suggested in *U.S. Navy,* a drybrush portrait of an African-American enlisted man with an authentic War of 1812 officer's tunic hanging on the wall behind him. Again, there is a strong sense of presence through absence, a kind of relaxed informality against a harsh and turbulent seafaring past that held no glory for African-Americans in the early years of our country's history. In terms of abstraction, Andrew Wyeth delights in the infinite variations of white and in the textures of wall and fabric. He uses the deep blue of the jacket and the sailor's dark flesh tones to create a kind visual ping-pong between the figure and background, thereby heightening the psychological tension and ironic juxtaposition in the otherwise cool and motionless portrait. The officer's coat, perhaps, has deep personal meanings as well: the artist's father, N.C. Wyeth, was working on illustrations for an edition of the Horatio Hornblower series when he was killed in a tragic train-car accident in 1945, just as Andrew was beginning to claim his own career as an artist. The cover illustration for one of the Hornblower books, with a figure wearing a similar jacket, was completed by Andrew shortly after his father's death in what must have been a wrenching posthumous collaboration. It would be the last illustration commission that Andrew Wyeth ever accepted.

The officer's jacket reappears in *Dr. Syn,* among Andrew's most unexpected and startling works. The title refers to a favorite Wyeth film starring George Arliss, about a pirate who becomes a minister. It is also a self-portrait; the artist even had an X-ray of his skull taken for the figure. The setting, which resembles the gun deck of an early 19th-century English or American warship, is, in fact, the interior of the fog bell tower on Southern Island, as remodeled by Betsy Wyeth to serve as a studio for her husband. Andrew, in turn, presented *Dr. Syn* to Betsy for her birthday; she promptly hung it in the living room at Southern Island. While such playfulness is a Wyeth family tradition, the painting gains poignancy in light of the artist's reference to this literal mantle passed from father, N.C. (the jacket was originally owned by N.C.'s teacher, Howard Pyle), to son, Andrew (who has since passed it to Jamie, as seen in several recent works). Wyeth friend and biographer Richard Meryman recently observed, "[Andrew] Wyeth, using many objects and people, has continued to paint his father. N.C. remains a central, perhaps hourly, presence in his life. . .'My father is still alive,' he says, 'I feel my father all around.'"

There is, of course, a great deal more to Wyeth's art than this complex, emotional subtext of loss, coupled with a natural but no less terrible sense of freedom from his father's powerful influence. Still, absence seems to be a recurring theme in many of the Southern Island paintings, most notably in *Squall* and in *Battle Ensign.* The latter, in Wyeth's mind, came to be about his old friend Walter Anderson, who died while Wyeth was working on the painting. The ensign is seen reversed and tattered, a symbol of the sea and blood and fighting. Although some viewers find the gritty toughness of the image unsettling, Wyeth simply responds, "I liked it because it was wrong."

Just as the unpredictable is one of the hallmarks of Andrew Wyeth's paintings, so is wit and the possibility for multiple ways of seeing ordinary objects and places. *Southern Comfort* is a kind of triple entendre, with the family dog at ease in the house on Southern Island. Overhead is a carved wooden eagle by native Maine artist John H. Bellamy, whose symbol of national readiness watches over the sleeping dog. The cutting light from an

Southern Comfort,
watercolor, 1987

Andrew Wyeth

unseen source energizes the inanimate carving while the animal dozes comfortably in the shadows — a perfect illustration of Wyeth's ability to transform the prosaic through unexpected ways of seeing ordinary events, in this case through the play of light.

The Maine of ancient magic and witches, a recurrent theme in many of Andrew's works, is seen in *Flying High* and *By the Light of the Moon*, with shadowy figures in the window and at the door. There is also a disquieting sense of imminence in the unusual angle of vision of *Signal Flags*. Like a beached ship, the lighthouse of *Signal Flags* can be read as hunkered down and anchored to the granite ledge or sliding irresistibly into the sea, nudged from its birth by the stiff following breeze indicated by the frayed flags. Even the rocks seem protecting and threatening at once, sheltering the lighthouse from the racing wind or crushing it in some cataclysmic upheaval.

There is a charged atmosphere in these later paintings of Southern Island, in which wind, sea and, especially, light seem always moving and changing. Only the lighthouse appears relatively fixed and immutable. Gradually we see even the lighthouse heave and loosen itself, as in *Signal Flags* — Wyeth's anchor slipping in a rising sea of restlessness within the confines of the island, now pressing in on him and shrinking the freedom and space so important to his art. His work completed here, at least for the present, Andrew and Betsy would soon leave Southern Island with Jamie arriving shortly after their departure to make it his permanent home in Maine.

A different Southern Island Light is the subject of Jamie Wyeth's recent paintings. But, as noted by James Duff, director of the Brandywine River Museum, many of the same qualities of human endurance, the mutability of nature, solitude and quiet, wit and humor, and the universal significance found in the local and ordinary are also present in the younger Wyeth's paintings, even as his approach to art is profoundly his own.

His island is a place where reality collides with a world of myth and magic, strangeness and wonder. The narrow gulf separating the two is suggested by *Meteor Shower*, one of the artist's most enigmatic paintings. A scarecrow with a strange, bird-like, leather mask and the War of 1812 jacket (the same jacket in *Dr. Syn* and *U.S. Navy*) is silhouetted against the night sky and the lights of Tenants Harbor a short distance across the water. The creature seems to cock its head, as if it hears nature's fireworks in the sky overhead. A portrait of the artist and his uncanny gifts and strange craft? His isolation and self-imposed exile from those "normal" folks across the harbor? Like many of Jamie Wyeth's works, there is a mournful note of deep melancholy interposed with humor and self-deprecation.

U.S. Navy,
*dry brush watercolor,
1983*

Andrew Wyeth

Magic is implied in several paintings of pumpkins. *Lighthouse Pumpkin* and *New England Pie Pumpkins* recall Halloween, a favorite Wyeth family holiday, from the times when N.C. and the family would put on costumes and makeup to bring to life the stories and myths he illustrated. So, too, is the memory of N.C., the grandfather Jamie never knew who was killed shortly before Halloween, invoked with affection and humor in the raucous gathering of pie pumpkins before a door slightly ajar.

Signal Flags,
watercolor, 1987

Andrew Wyeth

Several years ago when "the storm of the century" was predicted to hit the Maine coast, Jamie and his wife, Phyllis, packed their car and hurried back from their Delaware home to Southern Island (despite warnings that coastal communities might be evacuated). The storm was less ferocious than originally predicted, but Jamie found that the light tower "screamed like a dozen Metroliners" as the wind raced through the lantern flues. There is a streak of wildness and testing limits, of life under extreme conditions, in Jamie's art. Therein, not coincidentally, lies the essence and history of lighthouses in Maine.

Increasingly Jamie spends long periods on the island throughout the year. He spent weeks waiting for fog, the subject of *Light Station*, and since he paints directly, he could only work for minutes at a time on the painting when the fog finally rolled in, because the palpable dampness would not allow paint to adhere to canvas. The final painting is, however, fiction: neither the lamp nor the figure (Orca Bates, who has modelled for numerous other paintings) were present in reality. The lamp — here represented by a zig-zag flash of yellow that quite literally gives this work an electric charge — has long since been removed; Orca was added from memory. Not since Whistler's *Battersea Bridge* has anyone captured in oils so convincingly the tangible stuff of fog, its caressing, contour-eroding thickness and tonal complexity.

Orca Bates appears in several other paintings including *The Wanderer*, *Lighthouse*, and *Screen Door to the Sea*. In *The Wanderer* and *Lighthouse*, Orca is also partly the artist's nephew Richard Mills and partly Wyeth's wife, Phyllis. Neither painting is a portrait of them individually; it is all of them. Although Jamie Wyeth considers much of his work to be portraiture in the broadest sense, here his models are generalized into composites. The wildness of Orca is combined with the strength and courage of his wife and the youthful self- assurance of his nephew. In *Lighthouse,* the figure

Lighthouse Garden,
watercolor heightened with varnish, 1993

Jamie Wyeth

of Orca-Phyllis-Richard stands unsteadily, with hair blowing in the foreground against a whipping, cloud-strewn sky, more out of cinema set design than nature (or the stylized skies of his grandfather's illustrations). The lighthouse itself seems to be slipping down the grassy slope. As the artist once remarked, "Everything is flying in this picture." Anchoring and stabilizing the entire composition is the thin reed of the flagpole on the far left. Without this element the entire picture might indeed fly apart. Pushing all sorts of limits — compositional, stylistic and in subject matter — Wyeth ultimately creates an emotionally powerful image reflecting the inner lives of his protagonists and through them a more universal statement about reality and illusion, human fragility and permanence.

Lighthouse
Pumpkin,
mixed medium,
1992

Jamie Wyeth

Variations on this theme can be found in several ravishing paintings of flowers and plants ranging from the potted vegetable garden in *Lighthouse Garden* to the brilliant irises near the light tower in *Bees at Sea* and *Iris at Sea*. All refer indirectly to the improbability of survival, much less beauty, found on this rocky, windswept and sea-battered island. In *Iris at Sea,* the fragile, sun-bleached flower struggles tenaciously to lift itself against the looming lighthouse, which alone endures beyond the fleeting Maine summer.

If the iris is a metaphor for survival and tenacity, then Jamie's recent portrait of Phyllis, *Southern Light* (1994), is one of his most direct and compelling paintings to date. Framed by the sturdy, ornamental detailing of the doorway to the bell tower and suffused with a golden light, Phyllis stands before us with quiet dignity, erect and proud in the manner of countless images in literature and art of New England women and the sea. It is a miraculous, loving portrait of beauty, inner strength and endurance through grace. If the presence of N.C. Wyeth lingers in both artists' depictions of the lighthouse, the indomitable spirit of Phyllis Wyeth is embedded in the very granite foundations of Jamie's.

Acutely aware of the long tradition of lighthouses and islands in Maine art, both Wyeths uniquely evoke the earlier, Emersonian ideal of spiritual communion through the smallest details of nature. The Southern Island paintings must also be viewed in the context of their extraordinary sense of place, although each sees this place quite differently, in terms of emotional tone and emphasis as well as style and technique. Moreover, theirs is a modernist sensibility of self-awareness, of a kind of fluid deliquescence between form and subject, and precise, charged emotional intensity. Indeed, the sheer number and variety of views of this particular island suggest parallels with a contemporary "serial" esthetic found in in DeKooning's "women" series and Robert Motherwell's "Elegies to the Spanish Republic," or even the multiple soup cans of Andy Warhol (whose portrait Jamie Wyeth has painted). For the Wyeths, repetition, or, rather, continuity and concentration of vision, is like the steady, insistent gonging of the bell buoy or the beaming intensity and sharpness of the tower light. It is, then, a matter of a particular lighthouse becoming a place of continuity with the American landscape tradition, of continuing self-discovery and connectedness to family, of revelation and emotional rescue, as well as, perhaps, a *cri de coeur* for contemporary life's loss of in-sight — possibly the truest metaphor for the long-dark Southern Island Light, now illuminating realms of the spirit and imagination, through the paintings of Andrew and Jamie Wyeth.

Bees at Sea — Study #1,
mixed medium on tan
Bristol board

Jamie Wyeth

Christopher Crosman is Director of the Farnsworth Museum in Rockland, which recently announced plans to establish a special Wyeth Collection Center to exhibit and house works from the personal collection of Andrew and Betsy Wyeth, including various Southern Island paintings and watercolors by both Andrew and Jamie Wyeth.

New England Pie Pumpkins, *mixed media, 1992*   *Jamie Wyeth*

By the Light of the Moon, *watercolor, 1987*   *Andrew Wyeth*

The Maine of ancient magic and witches . . .

Screen Door to the Sea, *oil on panel, 1994* *Jamie Wyeth*

Boarding Party, *tempera, 1984*   *Andrew Wyeth*

Light Station, *oil and day-glo enamel on board, 1992*   *Jamie Wyeth*

Squall, *tempera, 1986*   *Andrew Wyeth*

There is a streak of wildness and testing limits,
of life under extreme conditions. . . .

Meteor Shower, *oil and essence of pearl, 1993*   *Jamie Wyeth*

A portrait of the artist and his uncanny gifts and strange craft?
His isolation and self-imposed exile from those "normal" folks across the harbor?

Battle Ensign, *tempera, 1987*   *Andrew Wyeth*

Lighthouse, *oil on panel, 1993*   *Jamie Wyeth*

*. . . a more universal statement about
reality and illusion, human fragility and permanence.*

Flying High, *watercolor, 1987*   *Andrew Wyeth*

Dr. Syn, *tempera, 1981*   *Andrew Wyeth*

Southern Light, *oil on panel, 1994*   *Jamie Wyeth*

*It is, then, a matter of a particular lighthouse becoming a place of continuity
with the American landscape tradition, of continuing self-discovery
and connectedness to family, of revelation and emotional rescue. . . .*

Bill Curtsinger

Where the water comes from: lenticular clouds over Katahdin and the other mountains in Baxter Park are part of the cycle that makes the West Branch of the Penobscot a major source of hydroelectric energy.

COSTS AND BENEFITS

Tamed for industry and settlement, the Penobscot River binds together a region of Maine as few other natural features can

DAVID D. PLATT

Year-round water flows and spectacular scenery combine to make the Penobscot's West Branch a prime spot for white water rafting and fishing.

L**ONG AND NARROW**, Chesuncook Lake suggests its geologic origins: a lake in a valley carved out first by a melting glacier 10,000 years ago and later by the water of the Penobscot River in its annual spring rush to the ocean.

From its southern end not far from Baxter Park, the lake stretches about 20 miles to the northwest until it splits, near Gero Island, into Caucomgomoc Stream, Umbazooksus Stream and the West Branch of the Penobscot River.

Maine's third largest lake, Chesuncook is part of the chain of water bodies and drainages that together make up the Penobscot River. Virtually all the water in this 2,012-square-mile, downhill-flowing system ends up in Penobscot Bay and eventually in the Gulf of Maine.

Impressive as it is today, the valley that forms Chesuncook Lake must have been more striking 150 years ago. Then, its forested hillsides would have seemed considerably higher, at least to a person standing on the lake shore, because the water was 40 feet lower than it is today.

Chesuncook is a "flowed" lake, impounded by dams built at various stages in its history for different purposes. By design, the dams have changed the manner in which its water flows down through a large portion of the Penobscot watershed. More important, the energy and mobility created by harnessing this water have spawned industries and communities along the river, from Chesuncook's sparsely settled shores to the intensely developed waterfronts of Bangor and Bucksport — development that, not surprisingly, has affected water quality in the river and its estuary.

Subduing the wild Penobscot has brought many benefits. Dams and turbines on the river supply more than half the power needs of their owner, Bowater/Great Northern Paper Company, and reduce the company's need to make electricity from fossil fuels. Just downstream of Chesuncook Lake, the managed water makes possible a white-water rafting industry that earns its owners millions of dollars annually. The Penobscot's year-round flows have created an impressive landlocked salmon fishery in the river above Millinocket. There is a productive bass fishery in the calm waters of the river above Old Town, where more dams have slowed the river's flow and created conditions favorable to these fish.

Year-round river flows have bestowed still more advantages on communities downstream, including Millinocket, Medway, Lincoln, Old Town, Orono, Veazie and Bangor — all of which are able to dilute their waste water in the river. Until the passage of federal clean water legislation in the 1960s, municipal officials could (and did) point to the dilution as an alternative to expensive secondary treatment plants. Dilution even helps the sewage treatment systems that have gone into service since those days, by making it possible to discharge higher volumes of treated waste water (plus storm water in some cases) than would be possible if flows were low at certain times of the year.

At the same time, converting the wild Penobscot of pre-settlement days into today's managed watershed has largely destroyed the river's primeval character. Stretches of its riverbed have been dried out completely (upper Ripogenus Gorge and a section near Millinocket are examples); a mixture of insidious pollutants has contaminated the water itself.

When the State of Maine in 1994 warned pregnant women against eating the tomalley (liver) of lobsters taken from Penobscot Bay and other Maine waters, it was responding to the presence of a toxic pollutant — dioxin — that had reached the marine environment by way of chlorine introduced at paper mills and municipal waste water treatment plants, including several on the Penobscot River. Concentrations of mercury, another toxic substance, have shown up in the Penobscot's impoundments, including Chesuncook Lake. Both of these pollutants are associated with the river's long history of industrial use.

The costs and benefits of punctuating the Penobscot's long basin with dams and discharges — evening its flows year-round, creating impoundments, injecting pollutants, transforming its fish habitat — can be weighed against one another. When Bowater/Great Northern applied to relicense its dams in the late 1980s, it contended it had done more good than harm; others, including environmental organizations and agencies responsible for protecting fish and wildlife, were unconvinced and insisted on improvements. And by the end of a licensing process that lasted several years and cost an estimated $10 million, environmentalists and recreational users of the river had won concessions from the

Katahdin looms over the river.

Natural values alone would make this river significant, but geography, history and technology have given it a part in human lives, too.

company. The Penobscot would continue to be used for industrial purposes, to be sure, but the public would be in a position to use the river for more of its purposes as well.

ENGINEERING ON A VAST SCALE

When Chesuncook Lake is full it contains 45 billion cubic feet of water, making it the largest single piece of a system that holds, in all, 58 billion cubic feet. The term "system" is appropriate; the 19 dams, 31 electrical generating turbines and two paper mills on this portion of the Penobscot River (known as the West Branch) are all under the control of Bowater/Great Northern, which built or re-built them in the early years of the 20th century as part of an engineering effort of staggering proportions. Today the West Branch system is the largest privately owned hydroelectric development in the United States, and, some believe, the largest in the world.

The system is the creation of two visionary entrepreneurs, Garret Schenck and Charles Ward Mullen. Schenck, who had built International Paper's first mill at Rumford, raised the capital to start what was originally known as Great Northern Paper Company. In 1899, Schenck left IP and became Great Northern's first president.

It was Mullen who first saw the possibility of combining resources of water, fiber and the drop in water into a single system. An 1883 civil engineering graduate of Maine State College (now the University of Maine), Mullen recognized the area's potential for generating the electric power that would be needed to run a paper mill employing the new "groundwood" process — a mechanical, energy-intensive technology for converting logs to pulp.

Constructing the Houlton line for the Bangor and Aroostook Railroad in the early 1890s, Mullen had noted the

Penobscot River's remarkably sharp drop in elevation: more than 1,100 feet in the 130 miles from Penobscot Lake to Medway, where the East and West Branches join to form the main stem of the river. Together with ample supplies of accessible timber and good transportation (the ability to float logs downstream plus the new rail line) the potential for power generation made the area a natural for large-scale industrial development. In 1897 the Maine Legislature granted Mullen, Schenck and others a charter to develop hydroelectric power and build a paper mill at Millinocket.

The area thus consigned to modern industrial development was by no means pristine. Logging operations had begun on the West Branch in 1828, necessitating the construction of dozens of small dams so the logs could be floated downriver to mills near Bangor. A total of 137 different dams have been built on the West Branch and its tributaries since then.

A log-driving company was organized in 1846 and operated a "boom" on Chesuncook where logs owned by various companies could be sorted and sent downstream. The log cribwork dam that first "flowed" Chesuncook Lake was built well before the middle of the 19th century, a few miles upstream of the present dam at Ripogenus Falls. (This older lake was 20 to 30 feet lower than the present one and was used in connection with log driving, not the generation of electricity.)

"The Maine woods had been 'opened up' by the time Great Northern Paper Company began to cut pulpwood," notes a company history, "but this was in terms of the needs of the lumbering industry." The coming of groundwood paper technology, with its need for year-round water to generate electricity and its reliance on a steady supply of four-foot "pulpwood" rather than long logs, would transform the region. The river that once rushed and rose as the snow melted in the spring, then gradually dropped and formed quiet pools in summer, became something quite different: a series of ponds and lakes controlled by dams and filled to the brim each spring, and then drained down slowly in summer to maintain the river's steady flow. By autumn and certainly by early winter under this regime, the lakes are again low enough to accommodate another spring melt. What still looks like "wilderness" to some people is, in fact, a highly regulated system, carefully engineered for the paper industry's purposes.

PUTTING THE SYSTEM TOGETHER

"After breakfasting on moose meat," wrote Henry David Thoreau of his 1853 visit to the West Branch region, "we returned down Pine Stream on our way to Chesuncook Lake. . . just below the mouth of this stream were the most considerable rapids between the two lakes, called Pine Stream Falls, where were large flat rocks washed smooth, and at this time you could easily wade across above them. . . ."

Much of what Thoreau saw at the upper end of Chesuncook Lake disappeared when Great Northern built the present Ripogenus (or "Rip") Dam in 1915. Constructed as the company added two paper machines at its mill downstream in Millinocket, Ripogenus was the largest storage dam ever constructed privately. Engineers sited the dam at the foot of Ripogenus Lake, where it narrows into Ripogenus Gorge (the site allowed them to build a shorter, cheaper dam than they could have upstream). The new dam raised the lake level by about 27 feet, flooding out the former log-driving dam. The old dam still appears from time to time, when Chesuncook Lake is drawn down as much as 40 feet during the winter to make room for the spring melt.

Other relics of pre-flowage days are in evidence as well. Several years ago a researcher towed a side-scan sonar device the length of Chesuncook Lake, noting among other things a standing dead tree, totally submerged. The tree never breaks the surface, even though it is more than 50 feet tall and once grew on dry land. The upper end of Ripogenus Gorge is a remnant of earlier times too — it was used to drive long logs and pulp before the construction of Ripogenus Dam and the underground tunnel that diverts water from the gorge to Great Northern's McKay power station. The sluice built in 1915 to get the logs downriver from Rip Dam still stands on the north side of the gorge, but it is dry today, and only a trickle of water runs down the gorge itself above the powerhouse.

In terms of elevation, the West Branch system starts at Penobscot Lake in Prentiss Township on the Maine-Quebec border, 1,350 feet above the point where the Penobscot River's two branches join to form its main stem at Medway. A dam controls the level of Penobscot Lake, storing water until it's needed to sustain the system's flow. When the dam's gates are opened, water flows down Penobscot Brook, through Cheney Pond and a section of the South Branch of the Penobscot River, and into another impoundment, Canada Falls Lake. A dam at its outlet controls the flow into Seboomook Lake, a long stretch of water that skirts the north end of Moosehead Lake, headwaters of another great Maine river, the Kennebec.

Water from Seboomook (controlled by a dam there) flows into the West Branch of the Penobscot, which trends east and north for about 20 miles until it empties into Chesuncook Lake at the point

Ripogenus Dam raised Chesuncook Lake to its present level early in this century.

described by Thoreau. On it goes, through the gates and tunnel at Ripogenus (bypassing the upper gorge), through Great Northern's McKay power station and into the fast-flowing section of the river favored by rafters, camera-toting tourists and fishermen seeking landlocked salmon. It ends up in North Twin Lake, goes over another dam and through a second set of turbines. Next downstream are powerhouses at Dolby, East Millinocket and Weldon (on the main stem of the river). Except for a single generating station at Medway owned by Bangor Hydro Electric Company, the entire system is owned and controlled by Great Northern.

Not surprisingly, it takes a computer to manage all of this water efficiently. "The game is matching the load with generation, while minimizing oil use," explains Dave Preble of the company's Power Systems Department as he sits at a console in Millinocket. From here Preble can monitor the water in upstream storage, open and close some of the dam gates (dams at small ponds are still operated by hand), dispatch electric power from the turbines and respond to the needs of the two mills.

Assisting Preble in these tasks is the "EOS" or Energy-Optimization System, a computer program developed about 10 years ago to manage all aspects of Great Northern's energy system. "The EOS gives us real-time data on a continuing basis," Preble explains. According to the company it was the first of its kind in the world. It consists of a "host" computer and several remote computers that monitor various aspects of the system, "talk" with each other at one-second intervals, and update the system every 3.5 seconds. Rows of glowing monitors above Preble depict the generating turbines at McKay, the "bus bar" where electrical energy created at McKay joins the system, 35 miles of transmission lines, and the steam load at the mills. "Everything's interrelated," Preble says. On a September afternoon, the screens tell Preble he has 30 billion cubic feet in storage in Chesuncook Lake, 11.8 billion cubic feet in 12 small ponds.

DRY SHORES AND SAWDUST

The dams and turbines on the West Branch generate 55 percent of the power Great Northern needs to run its paper mills. Making the most of this water — which becomes available either as melting snow in the spring or as rain in the fall, and which would disappear downriver if it weren't somehow managed — has obliged the river's controllers to develop a regime of fill-ups and draw-downs. The time of year (dry or wet), the temperature (warm or cold), the demand for paper, the cost of alternative power, the needs of other river users: all of these factors determine how the water is used and whether Chesuncook Lake is high or low.

Compared with coal, oil or nuclear power, hydroelectric energy is "free," meaning once the dams are built, there's no monetary cost for the fuel. This characterization is misleading, however, because it ignores numerous costs associated with hydro development.

For years, engineers dropped the water in Chesuncook and the other upstream lakes and ponds from January to mid-March, then filled the system from mid-March until early May. The result is a 20-to-40-foot-wide zone around the lakes that can't support wetland vegetation or spawning fish because it's dry for part of the year. "A common attribute of reservoirs, including the Ripogenus impoundment, is that water levels fluctuate," noted the group of conservation organizations that "intervened" in Great Northern's re-licensing application for this portion of its system two years ago. "One of the major differences between natural lakes and reservoirs is the unstructured shoreline and littoral zone of reservoirs and the sparsity of littoral vegetation as compared with natural lakes." The annual drawdown of Chesuncook Lake is capable of "exposing and destroying thousands of acres in the littoral zone," the groups complained. Fish species most directly affected by Great Northern's drawdown regime, they concluded, were brook trout and whitefish.

Affected likewise by fluctuating water levels are wildlife species that depend on wetlands: shorebirds, bald eagles and furbearers such as beaver and muskrat. The latter are "essentially non-existent due to the large winter fluctuations that prevent them from reaching their food sources."

What the river might have looked like before log-drivers and engineers controlled the spring freshet and raised the summer flow is anyone's guess. Overall, suggests hydropower coordinator Dana Murch at the Maine Department of Environmental Protection, the pre-indus-

The time of year (dry or wet), the temperature (warm or cold), the demand for paper, the cost of alternative power and the needs of other river users determine whether the lakes in the West Branch system are high or low.

trial Penobscot above Bangor probably resembled today's Saint John River in northern Maine. In late May the north-flowing Saint John provides some of New England's finest whitewater canoeing; by July, as the saying goes, it is "a mile wide and an inch deep."

Just *when* a shoreline is allowed to dry out accounts for most of the environmental problems, and before Great Northern applied for new licenses for Ripogenus and several dams downstream several years ago, it experimented with a modified schedule of drawdowns designed to lessen the disruption. Instead of dropping the water from January to mid-March, it began holding water in the lakes until the end of April, then lowering it gradually during May, June and July. Lakes were allowed to rise in August, then dropped gradually until December.

This plan, the company contended in its license application, amounted to a sacrifice of 18.7 megawatt hours of electricity annually, necessitating increased purchases of power from outside the system. Over the 30-year life of the license, the company estimated, the change in flows would cost between $1 million and $4.1 million, depending on the market price of electricity. (In their comments, the conservation groups disputed Great Northern's cost estimates.) Nevertheless, the company made the change permanent.

The entire Penobscot watershed, including the West Branch, was first developed for the purpose of harvesting, floating, sawing and shipping timber. Bangor, the port at the head of deep-water navigation, was, for a brief time in the middle of the 19th century, the largest lumber-shipping port in the world. Supplying the vessels that came upriver to Bangor were dozens of water- and steam-powered sawmills whose effects on the river are still evident today: a large part of the river bottom between Hampden and Bucksport is still covered with bark and sawdust from these operations. This carpet of organic material is believed to be several feet thick in places and doesn't leave the river, explains University of Maine oceanographer Jim McCleave, because it is trapped at the point where outgoing fresh water meets incoming salt water from Penobscot Bay.

An interesting question is whether the dams upstream, by evening out the annual flow somewhat, have altered the salinity of the lower Penobscot or Penobscot Bay. Just where salt water meets fresh depends on the interaction of incoming tide and out-flowing fresh water — and the location of that point changes as the balance between fresh and salt water shifts. In mid-summer, when river flows are at their lowest, salinity is measurable as far upriver as Hampden. But when the river is high in the spring, the fresh water pushes the salt down to Winterport, a half-dozen miles downstream. Where the fresh-salt interface was in the days before dams is anyone's guess. (McCleave suspects the regime wasn't greatly different, pointing out that the Bay's watershed is vast and that only part of the runoff reaching the Bay comes down the river.)

When it swims upstream to spawn, an Atlantic salmon can jump about 10 feet into the air. Thus a salmon heading up the Penobscot in pre-dam days could get as far as Ripogenus Falls, reasons Ed Baum of the Atlantic Sea-Run Salmon Commission, the agency responsible for salmon restoration in Maine. Spawning runs of that length probably ended with the construction of an early dam at Old Town sometime in the 19th century. The Bangor Dam, built at the head of river navigation in 1875, didn't stop fish migrations, says Baum, because it wasn't high enough to stop the fish at high tide. Still, today's active salmon fishery on the river between Bangor and Veazie dates from the breaching of the Bangor Dam about 30 years ago, and when a developer proposed closing the breach and redeveloping the dam to generate electricity in the early 1980s, salmon fishermen opposed the project and were largely responsible for killing it.

The other well-known salmon fishery on the river relies on a different variety of fish: "landlocked" salmon from four Maine lakes that were probably introduced into the West Branch of the Penobscot a century ago. This fishery extends downriver from the lower end of Ripogenus Gorge to the quiet waters above Millinocket. While the pre-industrial Penobscot might have been capable of supporting landlocked salmon, Baum says, it's likely the upriver storage and controlled flows have enhanced this fishery.

The Commission has no intention of trying to restore Atlantic salmon to the West Branch, says Baum.

Mercury contamination is associated with reservoirs, including several along the West Branch downstream of Chesuncook, and should be included in the list of environmental changes associated with the development of the river. Fish sampled in North Twin and Millinocket reservoirs, where levels fluctuate, "showed a statistically higher concentration of mercury," according to the intervening groups, than fish in lakes in which levels don't change. In its re-licensing application, Great Northern didn't study mercury contamination in Chesuncook, although it did so at sites downstream. In their comments on the application, the conservation groups asserted that the heavily fished waters of the Penobscot below Ripogenus Dam "have the high potential of containing mercury-contaminated salmon in the sport fishery."

Since the days of President William Howard Taft, the first sea-run salmon taken at the Bangor Salmon Pool has gone to the White House.

Overall, water quality in the Penobscot is less of an issue today than it was 30 years ago, when impoundments and untreated waste water combined to lower the amount of dissolved oxygen in the entire river. As far as salmon are concerned, says Ed Baum, water quality is "now excellent in most areas." Low oxygen above the Mattaceunk Dam at Medway, near the juncture of the West Branch and the main stem of the river, is a problem locally, says Baum, but doesn't seem to affect salmon in the river downstream.

Finally there is dioxin, a contaminant notorious for its toxicity. A byproduct of municipal waste water treatment and chlorine bleaching in the paper-making process, dioxin can't be linked to dams and turbines. Still, it is one result of the Penobscot's industrial development, and because of its known presence in the marine environment, it should be included in any list of downstream effects.

Toxic equivalents (TEQs) for dioxin in lobster tomalley at the point where the Penobscot River widens into Penobscot Bay were the highest of all the sites checked for a state dioxin monitoring program in 1993. The discovery prompted state officials in February, 1994, to warn pregnant women, nursing mothers and women of childbearing age not to eat lobster tomalley. The discovery of high concentrations of dioxin in lobsters was "unexpected," according to the state

Department of Human Services, and the warning (which continues to be in effect) was "based on the principle that developing children are considered to be at highest risk for possible injury resulting from exposure to dioxin."

It should be pointed out that the bulk of the dioxin in the Penobscot is believed to originate at two mills, both of which operate bleaching facilities: Lincoln Pulp and Paper in Lincoln, and James River in Old Town. Bowater/Great Northern uses a groundwood process — more energy-intensive but less dependent on chlorine.

CONFLICTS

For years, subject to minimum-flow requirements imposed by the state and by the Federal Energy Regulatory Commission, Great Northern has maximized its hydroelectric system's ability to turn turbines. Sometimes it has done so at the expense of those who would use the Penobscot for different purposes, and battles have broken out between the company and fishermen, white water rafters, environmentalists and energy-efficiency advocates, most notably in the mid-1980s when Great Northern proposed a new dam at Big Ambejackmockamus Falls ("Big A"). The dam wasn't built, but the conflict over the river intensified, and it continues today.

What is perhaps most striking about the very complex body of water we call the

Penobscot is its resilience. The water that leaves Penobscot Pond near the Maine-Quebec border passes in and out of lakes and over dams, through tunnels and penstocks, down rapids and through marshes, around turbines and past several paper mills and waste water treatment plants before it gets to Penobscot Bay. Over the years it has been used and misused, fouled and cleaned up. Even if it is no longer "wilderness" in any accepted sense, the river supports impressive populations of wildlife, including both landlocked and migratory salmon. The river's entire length is bald eagle territory, and golden eagles are known to nest above Ripogenus. Harbor seals frequent the lower river. Pilot whales have appeared in Bangor. By tradition, the first sea-run salmon caught at the Bangor Salmon Pool each spring goes to the White House.

Natural values alone would make this river significant, but geography, history and technology have given it a part in human lives, too. More than any other Maine river, the Penobscot has been an engine for development, contributing to the livelihoods of the people who live near it. Connecting land and sea, fresh and salt, past and present, it binds together a region of Maine as few other natural features can.

David D. Platt is publications director of the Island Institute.

DANCING IN THE DARKNESS

A night aboard
STARLIGHT V
is a lesson in biology and teamwork

PHILIP W. CONKLING

ALFRED OSGOOD, herring catcher from Carver's Harbor, Vinalhaven, is a legend throughout the Gulf of Maine. Ever since fishermen began catching the silver-sided herring in the Gulf of Maine more than four centuries ago, no other fisherman has landed anywhere near the volume that Osgood has pumped out of the sea night after night, month after month, year after year. With hand-picked crews from this island town, Osgood roams the herring grounds off Seal Island in outer Penobscot Bay, to Halfway Rock and Jeffrey's Ledge off Portland, and up to Stellwagen Bank off Gloucester. Every fisherman in these ports and a hundred others in between is familiar with the name of his boat, STARLIGHT, and the legendary successes of her owner, captain and crew.

When STARLIGHT V, the fifth and largest of Osgood's herring seiners, made her initial appearance one day this past summer in Carver's Harbor and tied up at the old crab plant wharf, few people remotely aware of the pulse of the harbor could fail to take notice. From her white pilothouse forward, STARLIGHT's pale green hull sweeps aft to measure 72 feet overall, encompassing sufficient capacity in her six holds to pack 300,000 pounds of herring.

Fishermen will tell you that once you've fished for herring, it spoils you for any other kind of fishing. Unlike the fishery for cod, haddock, flounder and other groundfish, which depends on dragging an otter trawl net rigged with heavy bottom chain and massive roller gear that roils a cloud of sediment and sweeps up everything in its path, catching herring has always been a clean fishery.

In the Gulf of Maine, herring are caught in a variety of ways, but they have, until now, all relied on nets arrayed at the surface of the sea to catch herring when they rise in the water column at night to feed. Not only is this a less destructive means of catching fish, but the herring fishery has not been plagued with the other major environmental impact of dragging for groundfish — "by-catch," the large numbers of fish of the wrong size or species that must be thrown back dead and wasted. But now fisheries managers in New England are permitting an increasing number of large "mid-water trawlers" to drag for herring in the Gulf of Maine since the fish has been designated as an "underutilized" species. But some scientific observers believe that however abundant offshore stocks may be, inshore herring stocks are in jeopardy from these new large boats.

In earlier years, most herring were caught in weirs with nets attached in circular fashion to wooden piles to trap schooling herring, or in stop seines with nets that are strung across the mouths of coves after herring have come inshore to feed. But increasingly herring are caught by purse seiners, both large and small, that try to encircle a school of fish at the surface and then "purse up" the bottom of the net to trap their prey in a pocket of net.

Because STARLIGHT V is being joined by other boats the government is encouraging to get into this fishery, it seemed worthwhile to try to learn something about the status of the herring fishery from those who know it best.

Facing page: The heave and surge of a netful of herring is enough to pull even a large vessel down on her rail.
This page: Members of the Independent Seiners Association in the Gulf of Maine share catches that are too big for one boat to handle, rather than tolerate the waste of dumping dead herring overboard.

Circling a school of herring with 2,400 feet of 40-fathom twine takes a tense three minutes.

CARVER'S HARBOR, AUGUST 26, 1994

The sun is still a blinding bright orb in the western sky as the crew of STARLIGHT V slips her lines off Osgood's wharf inside Vinalhaven's busy harbor. Seventy-three feet long with a high bow and a long sheer aft, she glides into the dying southwesterly sea rolling into West Penobsot Bay. Jason Day, 29, Osgood's alternate skipper, is at the helm while Billy Guptill and a crew of four others, including two of Alfred Osgood's sons, David and Justin, are busy below checking the lines, nets, rings, bouys, hydraulics and miscellaneous gear that this modern and efficient purse seiner carries neatly on her stern. Alfred, Jason and the others of the crew have been fishing this fifth incarnation of STARLIGHT for less than two months since she was rebuilt and refinished from an earlier life harvesting mussels on Nantucket Shoals. There are still some bugs and fine points to be worked out.

A serene glow emanates from inside the the pilothouse as Jason adjusts the radar, dials the Loran coordinates, punches in the course for autopilot and monitors STARLIGHT's course on the electronic chart plotter. Last night Jason and STARLIGHT found some herring south of Monhegan and it is to this large region of the Gulf of Maine that we will return to take up the night's chase.

Billy shortly appears in the pilothouse to use the cellular phone to order parts for a compressor after checking all boat systems and attending to needs of the 12-cylinder Caterpillar 3412 diesel that churns deeply below. The engine room is spacious and spotless to boot, but to a visitor accustomed to casual fishing-boat housekeeping the galley is the real eye-opener; it too is well appointed and spotlessly clean, a hint of the kind of wordless pride that suffuses this collective enterprise.

It will take us almost six hours of steaming time to reach the herring grounds STARLIGHT will begin to prowl tonight, so at 4 p.m. most of the crew eat a quick supper of chicken pot pie and retire to one of the 10 berths scattered below decks. But the slow heave and roll of STARLIGHT in the dying southwesterly is too intoxicating, and late afternoon summer sun is too full and entrancing to admit sleep right yet, although anyone with any sense knows there is a long night ahead. When the sun slowly rolls over the western rim of this world and its glow is finally extinguished, there is time enough for sweet rest in the arms of a serene sea.

While most of the crew sleeps, Jason brings STARLIGHT in through Large and Little Green islands, up underneath Monhegan's dark cliffs, and out beyond the arc of her first order light, all the while monitoring the crackle of radio traffic from other herring boats alerting him to the possibility of herring further southwest. When STARLIGHT suddenly throttles back in the darkness shortly after 9 p.m., the crew members appear instantaneously out of nowhere and suit up in full foul weather gear. We are off Outer Pumpkin Ledge, southeast of Bantam Rock, and Jason is staring intently at the patterns of color on the forward scanning sonar. Jason, whom I've known since he was 14 or 15, has not volunteered much all evening, but now quietly observes, "This is the most fish I've seen in quite a little while."

The loom of instrument light arrayed around Jason casts an eerie glow throughout the pilothouse, as he begins recording STARLIGHT's slow turns on the chart plotter. The herring appear as a bright wall of color on the sonar, from the top of the water column to the bottom, which appears as red in the image, but the school is in water too shoal to deploy STARLIGHT's deep net, which is also the largest in the fleet.

Off to port and starboard the lights of four other boats bob and blink in the inky night and all warily circle the fish, the ledges and each other. Suddenly the radio crackles intensely and Jason responds with a few words, but no one who hasn't listened to such communication for half a lifetime could easily decipher either the message or its response above the din of diesel. Then STARLIGHT begins to move ponderously off to the northeast toward one of the other boats.

Fifteen minutes later we come up alongside the ANNA LISA, a 48-foot seiner out of New Harbor, and as Jason carefully backs down, the skipper of the ANNA LISA, Paul Paulino, hands the ends of his seine net to STARLIGHT's crew. In the pocket of his net we watch approximately 160,000 pounds of silver-sided herring flipping near the surface, which is more than Paulino can load aboard his modest-sized vessel, so he is proposing to *give* the rest of the fish away. I stare incredulously at Jason; he's going to *give* them away. . . ? Jason explains that recently most of the Gulf of Maine boats got together to form the Independent Seiners Association and that one of the things they agreed to do was to share catches that were too big for one boat to handle rather than tolerate the waste of herring dumped dead overboard. It is abundantly obvious that some of the notions we carry around about the nature of fishing enterprises are not as up to date as the innovative institutions that fishermen themselves have devised, at least for this fishery.

Before STARLIGHT can load, another boat, the SARAH MCKAY out of Port Clyde, comes alongside ANNA LISA's port rail and she too is loaded. After both the ANNA LISA and the SARAH MCKAY are loaded to their scuppers, STARLIGHT takes on some 400 bushels; at $8 per bushel, we have just received a $3,200 gift with little fanfare.

SHOOTING THE NET

Although the 400 bushels are gratefully received, it is a small contribution to the 3,000 bushels, or 300,000 pounds of herring, that STARLIGHT holds and needs to satisfy its markets ashore. Jason returns his gaze to the chart plotter, which has captured in multi-colored tones the circles on the sea surface he has earlier circumscribed while stalking a larger body of fish. STARLIGHT's net runs to an astonishing 40 fathoms in depth, and Jason needs an additional few fathoms of margin to avoid tearing the bottom out of this $140,000 piece of equipment.

When we return to the spot on the bottom that is deep enough to make a set, the question is whether the fish are still there, and if so how many. Earlier Jason has observed that in summer the herring congregate in loose schools; but after cold weather sets in in the fall, a small spot of fish on the image can fill STARLIGHT's holds. Meanwhile, on the stern, STARLIGHT's crew waits quietly in the dark. Two men are perched on the bug boat, the short, fast boat that will carry the twine in a large circle around the herring when and if Jason gives the word. Everyone else wordlessly waits with tense and watchful patience.

We circle round and round in the inky void. It is very disorienting to be constantly changing direction. Piloting a submarine may be more challenging, but as I watch the exercise, I tend to doubt it. For Jason to give the signal to release the net, STARLIGHT must be uptide of the fish to avoid fouling the net in the propeller as it shoots off the stern; the fish must be in 45 to 50 fathoms of water to protect the net; the sonar signal must indicate a large and dense enough bunch of fish to make the set worthwhile; the location of other boats must be kept track of; the compass heading must be remembered; the movement of the feeding fish as they graze on the floating zooplankton pasture must be factored in; and no noise must spook the twitchy school. It is apparent that few people are equipped to keep all this information in mind at once, much less constantly updated as one or more of the variables changes, and why, in spite of all the wonder of the electronics, a set often fails to produce fish. Soon a half moon will rise, which makes the fish more uneasy at the surface, and Jason begins to monitor this too. It is abundantly clear why captains, in addition to their responsibility for the safety of the crew and vessel, receive a larger share of night's returns.

After slowly circling for well over an hour of intense concentration, Jason swivels in his chair, takes the mike that is wired to a speaker on deck and quietly says but two words, "Let's go." The brake on the winch cable holding the bug boat up on the stern lets go with a rifle-like crack, and then it all comes down to how quickly this small vessel can haul 2,400 feet of 40-fathom twine in a long arc around this body of fish before they spirit off, down or away. Perhaps three minutes pass before the leading ends of the net are handed up over the rail and Jason hastens back to the sonar. A slow smile spreads over his face as he peers at the sonar image of a bunch of fish neatly circumscribed on the screen. A whole village's worth of halogen lights goes on, as the bottom of the net is pursed and we gaze out at two acres of white corks lazily floating on the surface.

Jason goes down to the main deck to run the winch that once mangled his hand. The winch is connected to the power block on a gantry up over the stern that hauls the net back fathom by fathom. The crew gathers at stations on the stern to "flake" the net — Billy collects the rings, one by one, that draw the bottom of the net together to give it its name, and resets them on the needle, while the floats are piled off to port and the main body of the net is flaked carefully in between. Everything is made ready for the next set with an economy of motion and a brevity of quiet words that define the essence of teamwork.

As the net dries up, the herring flipping in the net make a sound like that of a hard rain and the heave and surge of this massive school is enough to pull STARLIGHT down on her starboard rail. It's hard to imagine the collective mind and body of this massive school rolling a boat the size of STARLIGHT down, but larger schools caught by smaller vessels have often been let go to avoid capsizing. As the herring flip in less and less water in the diminishing dimensions of the net, their scales, once collected for pearl essence for nail polish and other cosmetics, shine in the water, in the twine and in the drying pocket suffusing the whole scene in a kind of opalescent glow that is beauty itself. Meanwhile, just outside the net a pair of sleek shadows of seals cruise the perimeter of light, rolling lazily up for an easy feast on

Fishermen will tell you that once you've fished for herring, it spoils you for any other kind of fishing.

those herring that have flipped over the corks, but instinctively stay near the main body of the school. Moments later, out of the night sky, herring gulls also appear and swoop in for scraps. The mysteries of communication in the dark and deep are arrayed inscrutably before you, and you now know why they say this spoils you for other fishing.

The fish pump is lowered into the pocket of the twine. A waterfall of herring begins cascading into the first hold; this is quickly filled and the second and third shortly afterwards. Each of these six- to eight-inch adult herring weighs about a quarter of a pound, meaning there are perhaps 400 herring to a bushel; we have taken on several thousand bushels or a million individual silver-sided, blue-backed Atlantic herring in one set. It is an avalanche of herring, a bounty of the rich inshore waters of the Gulf of Maine.

After the lid on the last hold clatters back in place, Jason returns to the pilothouse and the elaborate dance begins all over again. Somewhere in the small hours of the morning, we make another set, and take on more herring. Then with her holds full, STARLIGHT turns slowly back toward Rockland, while everyone but Jason and Billy creeps happily into a berth.

CYCLES AND POLITICS

The night's haul is good news, not just for STARLIGHT, but for the complex web of interdependencies that this most basic of fish stocks supplies to lobstermen, canneries and smokehouses along the rim of the Gulf from Cape Cod to the Bay of Fundy. The bad news, however, along the Maine coast is that during the past year herring purse seiners such as STARLIGHT V (Vinalhaven), SARAH MCKAY (Port Clyde) and ANNA LISA (Round Pond) have been fishing in the same waters as an increasing number of large groundfish vessels. Last year vessels such as the WESTERN VENTURE and the ATLANTIC MARINER re-rigged for mid-water herring trawling, and they are now fishing on the same herring stocks as the seiners.

To understand why this is not simply another example of one fishing interest (seiners) complaining about incursions from another competing interest (mid-water trawlers) requires a basic lesson on the spawning biology of herring (which every fisherman knows) and an intimate knowledge of how our current fisheries management system works, or, as everyone knows or suspects, doesn't work.

For centuries, the vast abundance of herring in the Gulf of Maine has astounded fishermen, visitors and scientists alike; even the earliest reports from the region give a vivid picture of the importance of herring along the coastline of the Gulf of Maine. In 1675, the naturalist John Josselyn, who lived at his brother's plantation on the shores of Saco Bay, wrote, "The herring, which are numerous, they take of them all summer long. In 1670 they were driven back into Black Point Harbor by other great fish that prey upon them so near the shore that they threw themselves (it being high water) upon dry land in such infinite numbers that we might have gone half-way the leg amongst them for near a quarter of a mile."

Two hundred years later, the movements of herring from offshore areas in winter to local coastal spawning grounds around the rim of the Gulf of Maine had been described in careful detail. American fisheries biologist Spencer Baird wrote in 1877, "One principal spawning ground of the herring in the Bay of Fundy is near the southern head of Grand Manan; and by a very wise provision of the New Brunswick government, a closed [season] was enacted, extending from the 15th of June to the 15th of September, during which the capture of these fish was forbidden. They now resort to that portion of the coast in considerable numbers, and the quantity of eggs deposited is said to be something almost inconceivable."

This simple spawning area closure that Baird described more than a century ago was in effect for approximately 60 years dur-

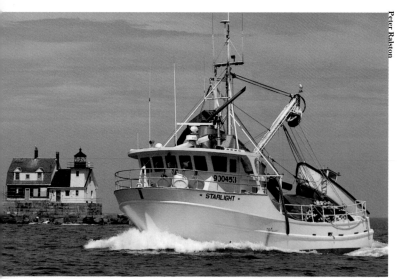

All five of Osgood's seiners have been named STARLIGHT.

Peter Ralston

Although Kaelin is at pains to point out that he is speaking as an individual, he goes on to say, "Mid-water trawling can take fish day or night; it's a more efficient way to catch herring, but the fish don't get a break. But the fish get a break from seiners when they are spawning on the bottom. Somehow we have to segregate the seiners and trawlers. If they fish on the same grounds, the trawlers will put the seiners out of business."

David Stevenson, the herring biologist in Maine's Department of Marine Resources (DMR), believes that the huge herring stock assessment numbers are "very conservative, overall. But we're talking about the whole Atlantic Coast. When we're talking about individual spawning populations in the Gulf of Maine, we really don't know."

Meanwhile Kaelin and others worry there is no regulatory means to limit domestic effort or prevent overfishing. The New England Fisheries Management Council is under tremendous pressure to respond to a variety of complex groundfish issues, including the closure of Georges Bank, and it is doubtful whether they can or will act. "We've got a real problem," says Kaelin.

A DAY'S BAIT FOR 100 MILES OF COAST

Hours later the chilly bleat of Owls Head Light foghorn registers in the deep folds of sleep. Outside a dripping fog clings to the twine and rails and to the spars of other vessels that are beginning to stir along Rockland's waterfront. Jason brings STARLIGHT in alongside Prock's granite pier beyond the ferry terminal at the north end of the harbor. Everyone looks lively again, though a tad less lively than the night before; lines are made fast, someone is dispatched to Dunkin' Donuts, while another member of the crew scrambles up the ladder to start the cranky fish pump, which will lift close to 300,000 pounds of herring up 30 vertical feet and into the fleet of O'Hara trucks that idle in a line above us on the wharf.

A small pickup is loaded first, in some kind of timeless waterfront ritual favor, and it hobbles off, down on its springs, the juice from a week's worth of fresh bait slowly draining out its tailgate. One by one the O'Hara trucks pull up under the shoot of the fish pump while thousands of pounds of lobster bait are steadily sucked out of the holds and dropped into their trailers. The first truck filled is bound for Stonington, but not before it is visited by a Rockland squad car solemnly reminding the driver to cover his load — more, one senses, to be a small part of this great scene than out of a real need to enforce a city ordinance in a seacoast town newly interested in tourists.

Somehow O'Hara seems to have cornered a good deal of the bait market for midcoast Maine and east to the Canadian border. Five tractor-trailer loads, plus the smaller haul of the WESTERN SEA, another purse seiner from which O'Hara buys, are just about enough bait to satisfy the August lobster market demand for a day. No wonder lobstermen think of themselves as mariculturists who feed Maine's population of lobsters.

The unloading at low tide will consume many more hours. Then STARLIGHT must still make stops at North Haven to unload bait, as well as stopping to resupply several lobster stations around the shores of Vinalhaven. A kind of weariness starts to set in as day and night and day begin to blur into one another. But it has been an undeniably good night; close to $24,000 worth of bait will be divided into shares, among Jason and the crew and STARLIGHT herself. And the weariness of the morning is nothing like that which sets in following those nights when the fish are elusive and their unhappy markets unmet. On this unforgiving coast, you must prove yourself every trip you take.

If Jason and the crew are lucky, they will get back to Carver's Harbor in time to see their families briefly, before resupplying and heading back out before the sun goes down. Billy Guptill and Alfred Osgood both have strings of lobster gear, if you can believe it, that they must find time to tend, now that these too are running wildly down the bay. But for these men, everything else is a sideshow when it comes to another round in the elaborate dance of a herring chase.

ing which time landings in this part of the Gulf of Maine, though they fluctuated annually, were reliable enough to support a major export industry of canned sardines and smoked herring. This provision for spawning area closure was dropped in the 1930s and Canada has since evolved a different management system based on an elaborate system of quotas, which has not prevented local population crashes. The Canadian system, like the American system and most so-called modern fisheries management, appears to have worked less effectively than those 19th-century measures that aimed at protecting important local spawning stocks.

For several hundred years we have known that herring aggregate in large schools and move onto spawning grounds in predictable patterns, first in Minas Basin and the Upper Bay of Fundy, then around Grand Manan Island, into Passamaquoddy Bay and along the eastern coast of Maine in the early part of the summer.

Spawning area closures are the primary management tool on the American side of the Gulf of Maine. Eastern Maine is closed to herring fishing for a month beginning August 15, western and central Maine for a month beginning September 1, and south of Portland for the month of October. For some reason Jeffrey's Ledge, an important spawning ground 50 miles south of Portland, is only closed for three weeks.

About a year ago, the National Marine Fisheries Service changed the method it uses to estimate herring abundance in the Gulf of Maine, basing the estimate on trawl surveys along the entire Atlantic Coast from North Carolina to southern New England and extrapolating abundance for the Gulf of Maine. And according to these surveys, herring stocks along the entire Atlantic coast are so large that the Herring Section of the Atlantic States Marine Fisheries Commission voted recently to increase dramatically the amount of fish that can be taken during the upcoming year. These same figures are also cited as the basis for allowing the shift of groundfish draggers to mid-water herring trawling. Although the robust status of herring stocks should be good news to Maine's herring fleet and remaining canneries, some of the industry's closest observers wonder whether the scientific numbers really add up.

Jeff Kaelin of the Maine Sardine Council (which represents canneries with boats now engaged in mid-water trawling) is increasingly nervous about the status of herring stocks and the increased fishing power on herring in the Gulf of Maine. "No one is finding fish right now," said Kaelin recently. "They don't see the signs of huge stock assessments." Herring purse seine captains are more blunt: they believe that trawling for herring disrupts spawning aggregations, breaks up the schools, takes more spawning adults, has higher by-catch, reduces the spawning potential, and will eventually devastate the resource.

Leighann Chilles aboard CRAIG AND KURT, where she is stern woman.

STERN WOMEN

"Mommy's gone out to haul"

KAREN ROBERTS JACKSON

When my husband, children and I first moved to an outer island, one of my prouder achievements was learning to handle our little lobsterboat ROSEBUD. Becoming a competent woman in a boat, landing gracefully at the dock, handling lines with one baby in a backpack and three other children in lifejackets, I relished an aura of capability. Relish does not come without initiation. I also screwed up many a time, guessed the wind and tide wrong, got seriously lost in the fog, nearly lost a kid or two overboard. But, when the first salute of acknowledgment finally came from the local fishermen, I waved back feeling smug and accepted.

Women on the water are not a common phenomenon on this coast. Women working on the water, sternmen in oilskins in all kinds of weather, began to intrigue me. A wave from one of them would give me a sense of kindred spirits. I have often likened island life to early pioneer life because of the ruggedness and isolation. Seeing women on the water was like seeing another woman on the long, dusty trail, or the great plains of Kansas. A welcome sight to a homesick rusticator.

I will admit I went at this piece with many preconceptions. Blame it on being "from away," but I guess I wanted to hear stories about feminist values and oppressed housewives. I wanted to hear about a righteous sense of equality. But, mainly, I wanted to know these women who wore mud boots like mine and often smelled of herring in the grocery store.

One woman in particular used to capture my heart. Often in a cove near my home I would see her sterning with her two sons. I loved the sight of her against the early morning red sky and wished I could capture a photograph of her. I loved the way "stern mother" sounded and tripped off my tongue; ditto "stern woman," "stern wife." Great images of gentle women with toughened hands.

So after more than a year, I screwed up my courage and asked if I could speak with a few of them. I was graciously invited to share a kitchen, a lunch, a beer, an afternoon. Each, in turn, took my preconceptions and blew them out of the water.

What follows are my conversations with these fine, stern women.

Jean and Jacob Thompson, mother and son, in front of the Vinalhaven Fishermen's Co-op.

Nora feels that if there is any advantage or asset to being female aboard a vessel, it might be in the area of neatness.

RUSTY AND TERRY WARREN, mother-in-law and daughter-in-law, are married into a Vinalhaven lobstering family. Terry, age 29, is sternman to her father-in-law, Charlie, aboard his boat SUNLOVER. Rusty, in her 50s and matriarch of this clan, runs the support system on the home front. In the spring of '94 the family purchased two new Novi boats, one for Charlie and one for his son Ira, Terry's husband.

From April to October (prime lobstering season on Vinalhaven) Rusty's day begins at 5 a.m., with a sacred half hour all to herself before her man arises. She uses the time to stoke the fires and to pack the "dinner pails" for Charlie, Terry and Ira. She turns on the VHF to check the weather channel and to hear what the conditions are like from the few hardy souls already out. Around 5:30, the family is meeting in the kitchen, engaging in what is locally known as "lobster talk."

Rusty describes the scene: "It's how we start the day. A cup of coffee, then the men discuss where to go . . .'Up to Easter, or Seal?' 'I got six strings at Brimstone, think I'll move them to three fathoms.' The men talk it out and plan their day. They have their own names for everything, Charlie's got a different name for all the grounds — 'bander bottom,' 'old woman's ass,' 'the California piece . . .' We talk about the weather for the day. I try to think up something interesting for their dinner pails, something a little different for when they are out there."

Once the adults are sufficiently fed and coffeed up, Rusty drives them down to the bait dock, usually taking a moment to watch the day come up before returning to roust Ira and Terry's three children, Amber and Amanda, age 7, and Ira, Jr.,

age 6. They will spend their day on Grandma's heels, either in the garden or chasing chickens or baking bread. Their parents, most nights in the summer anyway, won't be in from hauling until seven or eight o'clock. Then they will end their day at the supper table together.

Says Rusty, "We have a family connection, we all share the work, and who's ever ashore just does it."

Rusty tried her hand at sterning for Charlie, but literally, did not have the stomach for it. The going round and round in circles that a lobsterman does while hauling in traps made her queasy. Try as she might, she did not have the physical strength to "break" a trap on board. That was when Terry agreed to give it a try. Charlie and Terry haul 200 traps a day, putting in 12- to 14-hour days in the summer.

With admiration, Rusty states, "Terry proved right off she could do a man's job. She could bull the traps around, keep ahead on the bait bags, whatever. The captain's job is to set the pots, he knows where to put them, looks for good bottom, he's got the science of it, the thinking part. But, once the trap breaks aboard, it's the sternman's job to measure [the lobsters], sex them, punch them, throw out the crap, band the lobster, rebait the trap. If you are hauling a string, you can have as many as six traps lined up on the washboard . . . but Terry can keep up real good."

Why does Terry stern for her father-in-law rather than her husband?

Says Terry, "You work a lot harder for someone else. The captain expects a sternman to keep up, you can't get away with stuff the way you would with your husband. If you are with your husband you bring all the stuff from home, or you get real tired and say to him, 'You do it, you haul that damn trap.' You get less work done and you catch less lobsters. Charlie and I talk a little, but not much, it's too busy. Some days we are silent all day."

Terry recalls being sick one day during the season: "I went to haul anyway. I just puked between strings."

She recalls another time going overboard to retrieve a trap that was in water too shallow for Charlie to approach; "it had three lobsters in it, too."

She also remembers the time a lobster nipped her, causing her to flinch and toss the bander overboard; "I banded for the rest of the day with my fingers, 200 pounds of lobster."

With my own self-righteous leanings, I expected Terry to have plenty of reason to gloat over her abilities and her earnings, her proving herself in a man's world. Lobstering is good money for a woman on an island, especially with such a seasonally dependent economy. Terry is able to see her earnings in the renovations to their home, the new bathroom, the paid bills, the school clothes for the children.

Nevertheless, in her own words, Terry says, "It makes you appreciate more what your men have to do. It made me appreciate the nights that Ira got home ahead of me and had a fire going for me. It makes you a lot more careful in how you spend the money, knowing how hard the work is to get it."

Rusty's involvement encompasses more than filling dinner pails, having supper ready and tending children. When it became evident that she was not cut out to be a sternman, she threw her ambition into the entire spring haul-out, single-handed, of SUNLOVER, sometimes with grandchildren in tow. As Rusty describes the job, you can see her going over every square inch of that 35-foot wooden boat in her mind. Just her litany on fitting out a boat leaves you exhausted.

"Well," she says, "it's simple. You have to scrape, sand and paint the entire boat from top to bottom, starting with the canopy. The boat looks so huge in the boatyard; usually half of it is underwater, but in the yard you are up there 10 to 12 feet off of the ground! I didn't get the whole thing down to bare wood, and I couldn't just scrape the whole boat, then sand the whole boat, it was too overwhelming, so I worked in sections. First you're on the trunk, then the coamings, the bow, washboards, scrape inside and out. I must have gone into the wheelhouse after that. You verathane the wheelhouse so the gurry will wash off. Then scrape and paint the starboard and port bulkhead, then around the electronics, every nook and cranny. Then you lay down on deck to get beneath the coamings and the washboards. Then you go from the inside to the bottom, to copper the bottom, then the name. I had to keep jockeying the truck around so I could stand on the truck. Charlie likes to have pine tar on the deck so it's sticky, not slick. It took me one month, you had to let it dry in between coats and we had so many foggy days. I was the only woman in the boatyard, I felt so slow compared to everyone else. On all the other boats three or four guys would get on a boat and they would have her overboard in a day or two."

When I ask her what she thought her labor came to in dollars, she says, "Oh, I probably saved Charlie about a thousand, but if you write that, you'll have every fisherman's wife being asked to do the haul-out! I do it willingly, I like to work with my man. I kept thinking, Jesus, I have got to get this finished so Charlie can get out to haul."

When Rusty can be caught in the house, she keeps an ear to the radio. She vividly remembers the day Ira hit a ledge; no big deal, but on the way in he began taking on water. When Charlie and Terry got into the harbor with no sign of Ira, they went back out to check on him. He had the boat at full speed and was pumping like mad. Terry jumped aboard to help with the bailing and they just reached Hopkins' Boatyard in time. Rusty listened to the whole episode with a choked throat.

Says Rusty, "I keep on the radio all the time. I think of all the mothers, wives and grandmas listening for their men on the water. I don't take any day for granted."

Both Rusty and Terry downplayed the extremes of their work on the water. They assured me that if I wanted to talk to a rugged offshore woman, I should speak to Nora Warren, another daughter- in-law/sister-in-law, married to Ira's brother Jimmy, and expecting their first child. Nora, they told me, had gone gillnetting for two years before becoming a sternman for three more.

For a woman to have gone gillnetting offshore, staying out for several days at a time, was another challenge altogether.

An off-islander, Nora began coming to Vinalhaven several years ago on her summers off from Boston University, where she studied theatre and stage management. She says she grew up in a setting where male versus female was never an issue. "There was never any reason why I couldn't do whatever I wanted to do," she claims. "In the theater, too, if you could do it, whether it was carpentry or stage lighting, it didn't matter. When I came to Vinalhaven, there was nothing else to do to make any real money. I thought it would be fun to go fishing, I didn't really think about being the only woman."

Nora admits she "just walked up and asked for a job" with Jimmy Poole aboard his 42-foot gillnetter. She was taken on as crew with three, sometimes four, other men, fishing the waters some 60 miles offshore.

Nora, age 29, described the work as not so much strenuous but requiring a good deal of stamina, a long day spent coiling rope, dressing fish and flaking the nets. At first she was allergic to the "belly stuff" in the fish, and broke out in sores. But she liked working for Jimmy, calling him a "hard worker" and a safe captain who ran a safe boat. Her relationship with the other crew members was one of mutual respect.

Says Nora, "The guys would have cut me a break if I had asked, but I never asked. They always treated you fine. You never really stop for lunch or take a break. We used to feed each other sandwiches while the other two were flaking the nets. You talked and kidded all the time; it got to where you only had to tell the punch line of the joke."

The gillnetters' hours, more than the physical work, eventually led Nora toward a sternman's position. "It was such a strange schedule," she explains. "You would head out at 1 or 2 a.m., sleep on the way out until 5 a.m., and then stay out for two or three nights."

Later she smiles and adds, "I would never have met Jimmy [her husband] if I had stayed gillnetting, not with such a crazy schedule."

After a summer off, Nora went to work with lobsterman Steve Rosen on his vessel WILL O' THE WISP. Steve, says Nora, is

Nora Warren

Terry and Rusty Warren in Rusty's kitchen, where the action begins shortly before 5 a.m.

"You begin to know almost everything about one another when you spend 12 to 14 hours a day, five days a week, eight months a year."

another hardworking captain who runs a safe boat.

Speaking of the integrity of both captains, Nora comments, "I can't say enough about what it is to work with men who are proud of their boats, concerned with safety, and also men who want to get home to their families, want to get in in time for supper. I'm pretty spoiled about that now."

When asked about her ability to step in if ever an emergency arose, Nora answers, "I thought a lot about that and sometimes, on foggy days, I never knew where we were. But, I could understand Loran and radar and how to handle the boat itself, and I felt that if I had to step in, I could do it."

Nora feels that if there is any advantage to being female aboard a vessel, it might be in the area of neatness. "On a boat, you do things the same way, every time, always the same, and you can't do it fast enough. So the neater it is, the easier, the faster. That might be a place where a woman's touch comes in."

Asked about a woman's tendency toward nurturing, Nora responds, "Well, you always share your lunch, or trade things, and I'd make cookies with fewer chips because I knew Jimmy liked fewer chips, stuff like that. In truth, you spend more time with the captain than the captain spends with his own wife and that is a little different, being a woman, but it has never been a problem. A captain may confide feelings and emotions with a sternman, like a buddy or a chum. You begin to know almost everything about one another when you spend 12 to 14 hours a day, five days a week, eight months a year. You get comfortable with one another because you are working really hard, you

see each other exhausted. You can have terrible days when you are disappointed and aggravated with each other, but you get over it pretty quick because [on the boat] there is nowhere else for you to go."

Nora agrees that it is not a good idea to go fishing as husband and wife, saying it is hard on a couple to spend that much time together. Nora's husband, Jimmy, is also a sternman as well as a carpenter. "Lobster talk" makes up a good deal of their dinner conversation and they tend to keep an eye out for one another while on the water.

Nora asked her husband if he would set up a daughter with a boat, traps, gear and such just as he would a son. His reply was, "Certainly." He added that it would not bother him at all to have the harbor's first female captain for a daughter.

While admitting that a sternman's share is good money for a woman, Nora wonders how families supported solely by a sternman's pay can make ends meet.

Says Nora, "You can say that you make $350 a week year-round, or that you make nothing and sometimes you make a thousand, either way it is not a very secure profession. Even so, I took this summer off before the baby [due in February], and it cut our income in half. Even though I worked nearly every day at either child care or waitressing or catering, it is not the same. In a restricted community there is not a lot of choice for anybody, even less for a woman. It is hard work. You go when the captain says 'Go.' The captains don't always want to go, but they do. You might as well be cheerful about it."

Economics played a large part in Leighann Chilles's decision to become a sternman. An off-islander married to an islander, the 26-year-old woman is mother to a 16-month-old son and a three-year-old daughter. She and her husband, Shawn, are working to build their first home.

Says Leighann, "I can't do any other job and also afford to pay a babysitter. I used to work for General Electric, in a really responsible position. I would work all week long and make $190 — I make that in a day of lobstering."

When I visited Leighann, it was at the end of her (so-called) work day. She had gotten home in time to grab a shower. In between talking with me and answering the flow of questions and needs from two gleeful toddlers, she was preparing dinner. She had started the roast in the crockpot at 5 a.m. but forgot to turn it on in her rush to get out the door. Nonplused, she was now switching to the pressure cooker and soon had it hissing away.

Leighann's son Tyler was born in mid-June and she was back sterning by mid-July. She has hired a younger sister to care for the children during the day.

She says, "I knew if I was going back, I had to do it soon, before I couldn't go back. I love my children and I love being with them, but somehow I always knew that I would want to work as well."

Leighann sterns for Sonny Warren, aboard the CRAIG AND KURT. As with the other women to whom I spoke, the relationship between captain and sternman has proved to be ideal.

She explains, "I am quite lucky to be going out with Sonny, I don't know if I could do it with anyone else. He is very understanding of my position. Sonny likes to head in around 3:30, which helps a lot. If I need to come in earlier, he will do it. If I need to take a day off because of my kids, he understands and we make it up another day."

Also, like the other women, Leighann feels a mutual respect between herself and Sonny. "Sonny and I can talk and joke and we know it won't go any further than the boat. We really trust one another and I feel lucky that way, too."

Leighann grew up in the Adirondack Mountains of upstate New York, which, she says, makes her position a bit unique.

"I wasn't brought up here, and I wasn't brought up around boats or around the water. Fishing did seem a rather man-oriented thing, I wasn't sure I could physically keep up. The hardest part is the lifting. I feel it more in my body now, especially since I have had another baby. Sonny told me when I first came on that 'I didn't think you'd make it,' but I have been going with him three years now.

"I do a man's work, keep the house and take care of my kids. I get pretty tired and cranky sometimes, but in some ways I feel it makes me a better mom. My kids are used to the routine now, Olivia will even say, 'Mommy's gone out to haul.'"

For Jean Thompson, the stern mother who first caught my eye, going lobstering with her sons, Jacob and Murray, was just one more aspect of her role as a mom. Four summers ago, when the boys were 10 and 8, Jean helped her sons procure a 19-foot open boat equipped with a hauler and a 75-horsepower outboard. The boys pooled their savings accounts for the down payment and committed themselves to a yearly payment each August 1. This year they paid their debt in full.

With 25 traps donated by their lobsterman father, who fishes offshore, a few lessons aboard their grandfather's boat, and a diligent stern mother, the boys started out in business. By the end of the first summer they were up to 40 traps, mostly in and around the harbor and the Reach. This last summer Jacob bought out his younger brother, bought a new engine, Loran and VHF, and increased to 200 traps. He and his mom moved further offshore, out and beyond Hay Island.

Says Jean, "Going with them was the only way to keep an eye on them. I had also been told that in order to run anything over 9.9 horsepower, you had to be 16 years old."

Jean does not take the usual one-fifth cut that is the average pay of a sternman, explaining, "I just wanted them to earn it." A teacher for 20 years in the Vinalhaven school system, Jean goes out to haul with the boys from June to October. Depending on the weather or how tired they are from school and sports activities, they check their traps two or three times a week.

Jean says, "We get up real early, go down and have breakfast with the fishermen, and try to get done by one or two o'clock. In the fall we haul after school. Sometimes it is hard because you want them to be kids, to be able to play soccer and stuff if they want to."

Asked if they always get along amicably out on the water, Jean replied, "No. Murray gets nervous sometimes, and Jacob is the boss, the captain. I just do my job."

Around this home, too, the conversation is often "lobster talk." Jacob will ask his father's advice on where to shift his traps. Jean says her husband, Frank, will always put the question back to Jake, asking him what he thinks is the best plan.

Says Jean, "I know a lot more now than I did when I started, I can carry a conversation now."

Out on the water the mother and her sons exist in a somewhat different relationship, one probably enviable to many parents in today's society. Mother and sons have been in a couple of tricky situations in an open boat, in fog and rough seas, that required mutual calm and reliance. Other times the conditions have created the perfect setting for deeper conversations of a different sort.

Jean reflects, "It is a lot of work and commits a lot of time. I have always done a lot with my boys because I believe you can never get those years back. When we are out there we get to really talk, we get in a lot of great discussions that we might not have otherwise. Even though Jacob is 14 now, he still spends a lot of time with me. We still get to cutting up and kidding around, Jacob still likes to try to get water down my oilskins."

I asked Jean if her boys ever express their appreciation for the time she spends working with them. Jean says, "They don't really say it, they don't have to; I know they do. Oh, sometimes after a good day we will come in and Jacob will say, 'I will treat you to lunch, Ma.'"

Each of these women gave me a tidbit to ponder — about island life, being a wife, raising children, earning a living. We discussed how it is neither a female or male attribute to wonder at the glory of a sunrise, the black and white stark beauty of winter on the water, and to feel humbled by witnessing ocean creatures and birds in their own environment. I, too, have a 13-year-old son who is a sternman, and I, too, want him to be a child as much as possible. More than all that, these stern women invoked in me a clearer sense of what it is to be a strong, yet serene, island woman. I am very grateful.

A resident of Vinalhaven and Greens Island, **Karen Roberts Jackson** *contributes regularly to Island Institute publications.*

Illustration by Siri Beckman

BRIMSTONE

THERE ARE EVENTS, few and far between, that have an incendiary effect and burn in the mind like a fire gone underground. Most of these were lit unexpectedly for me on the far headlands of remote islands, and occasionally the reflection of their glow assembles on the backside of the skull, to serve as a reminder of just what it is on this coast that keeps one turning to the east, to those far hills cut off by a rising sea some eon ago.

I spent the 1975 summer field season as an intern for The Nature Conservancy, careening among a dozen islands — some remarkable, some not — in earnest collection of facts. Species lists of plants, inventories of intertidal invertebrates, notes of songbirds, counts of seals, habits of seabirds, descriptions of rock types, these filled the notebooks — as if you could arrive at the universal nature of island life from an induction of catalogued observation.

The notes from that time, those islands, freeze-frame events in their various cycles from fullness to failure of large or small moment, punctuated from signs left by the beast that walks upright — the furtive deer herd on Bradbury Island (which thrived), the tentative tern colony on Smith Island (which failed), the ground nesting osprey on Sheep Island (which moved), the Indian shell heaps on Big Garden (which diggers damaged), the heron colony on Mark Island (which eagles displaced), the tombolo beach on Goose Island (which the sea reshapes, every tide, timelessly).

But one or two events from those years of observation burn down through the years, down through layers of consciousness to deeply buried places of the mind. It is here, in these inner sanctuaries, that the essence of islandness has shape and form.

As the summer of 1975 drew to an end, I got the opportunity to spend a day on Brimstone Island south of Vinalhaven which I had heard about from almost the first day I arrived in Penobscot Bay.

FROM A JOURNAL ENTRY:
Brimstone Island: August 28, 1975. Out beyond the ragged southern fringe of Vinalhaven are a half-dozen islands in a group, all treeless and burnished a tawny gold in the late summer sun. I have the day on the largest of these islands, Brimstone, named for its beautiful, peculiar bedrock, which pokes like dark bones from beneath its thin skin of heath. Brimstone's bedrock has been quarried into a billion tiny pieces by pounding sea and prying ice and is piled onto a pair of steep cobble beaches on either side of the island where on a calm day you can land and prospect for the indescribably smooth blue-black lucky stones which the sea's swash has polished to a high sheen. With a little oil from the nearly vestigial gland beside your nostril, you can add a three-dimensional luster to a brimstone and if you can find one without so much as a hairline fracture you have a lucky piece as old as time itself.

As I ascend the high hill overlooking the beach where the peapod looks incongruously small, all of Penobscot Bay is revealed. Seventy fat seals are hauled out in the morning sunlight on a skerry off nearby Little Brimstone and gulls slice by overhead on the updrafts which sweep up the cliffs from the sea. I have read that a rare nocturnal seabird, no bigger than a robin, called the Leach's storm petrel, nests on a few of Maine's offshore islands and want to find out if Brimstone is one of them. I cross to the outer shore of Brimstone and start to climb down one of the cliffs toward a little beach below. The outcrops get steeper with only a narrow ledge for footing and as I edge my way along, face to the cliff, hands reaching for a grip, I run out of ledge at a crevice which I cannot cross. I am about to turn back when I am startled to see a crow staring at me across the crevice at eye level, about four feet away. For a minute or so, neither I nor the crow moves. Something is wrong; there is no nest in sight, so why is the crow motionless? As I start to ponder the thought, the crow takes off, beating one wing furiously, while trailing a useless broken wing behind. It careens downward like Icarus and lands a few hundred feet out from the base of the cliff, wild dark feathers scattered in the sea. Within seconds, a gull flying in toward Brimstone cuts a tight circle and shrieks above the crow, which is now trying to paddle away with its one good wing. In three more seconds the gull is joined by several others — large black backs and gray herring gulls — which swoop and stall above the crow on steep downward glides. The shrieks of the gulls, which soon number a dozen, are met by an eerie cry of the crow, which knows the gulls mean to kill it. The crow on its back faces the sky from where its tormentors come; it rises up out of the water, beak first, to parry the dlives of the murderous circling gulls. Then two gulls work in a pair; as one swoops in toward the crow that again arches itself up, another hits it from the back, breaking its neck. The horror is over. The crow, a limp, dark thing, looks like a spot of oil in the morning sunlight, with a blue black fading sheen, it is for a few more moments the color of sea-worn brimstone. The gulls do not even eat it.

So long as I live, I will never forget the sound the crow made to drown out even the shrieking cries of the gulls. But it was also without remorse, without any quality except the purest essence of wild defiance. I will carry this sound in my inner ear to the grave.

In recollecting these island voyages, I now know what I did not then: that the power of these places transforms the very nature of people — even of occasional visitors like myself. And the longer we stay, the deeper the transformation; rocks we once thought dumb, sing; birds dance; seals outwit us; spruce groans; and the sea keeps wrapping us in its arms, dissembling everything.

— *Philip W. Conkling*

"REMOVED"

How Sutton Island lost its year-round community

CARL LITTLE

"BIG ISLANDS ARE always attended by little islands, like sharks with their pilot fish," wrote Maine island chronicler Dorothy Simpson in describing Mount Desert and its attendant archipelago, the Cranberry Isles. The five fish — Great and Little Cranberry Island, Baker, Bear and Sutton — lie off the southern end of the big island, which half encircles them with its range of hills.

At roughly 175 acres, Sutton — or Sutton's or Suttons, depending on who's saying it or writing it out — is the third largest of the Cranberries.

"An island about a mile long," was Charles Eliot's reckoning of Sutton in his classic *John Gilley: Maine Farmer and Fisherman* (1899), "which lies between the Cranberry Islands and the island of Mount Desert, with its long axis lying nearly east and west." Later surveyors put it at about a mile and a quarter long by a half mile at its widest. Whatever its precise length or width, Sutton has all the dimensions — historical, physical and literary — of a remarkable island.

Until a definitive history appears, the fullest accounts of Sutton can be found in Charles McLane's *Islands of the Mid-Maine Coast, Volume II: Mount Desert to Machias Bay*, and in George Lyman Paine's informal *Sutton Island Maine: Its Houses, People, Animals, Weather* (1963). The accuracy of the latter has been questioned by some, including Samuel Eliot Morison, the eminent sailor-historian and author of *The Story of Mount Desert Island* (1960), and it is reported that Admiral Morison once delivered a half-hour critique to Reverend Paine, detailing everything his friend had either got wrong or overlooked in his book on Sutton.

The naming of the island can be traced back to 1757 when Ebenezer Sutton of Ipswich, Massachusetts, in the company of Gloucesterman Abraham Somes (who went on to found Somesville), received a deed to the island from the Indian "governor" of Mount Desert Island in exchange for two quarts of rum.

Sutton Island was eventually purchased by William Bingham of Philadelphia as a part of his vast holdings. Bingham slowly sold off his holdings to settlers, although Thornton reports that his estate was still paying taxes to the Town of Cranberry Isles in 1938.

Census schedules record the waxing and waning of the island's year-round population. Beginning in 1830, the year Sutton became a part of the Cranberry Isles township, four families comprising 20 residents lived on the island. Sutton peaked in population in 1860, when 11

John Gilley homestead, Sutton Island. Gilley settled in Sutton in 1854 and drowned in 1896.

families, which included 43 individuals, made their home there. After that, a gradual decrease occurred; by the year 1900, year-rounders consisted of five families and 27 residents.

The best account of life on the island in this period is found in Eliot's *John Gilley*, the first volume of the "True American Types" series published by the American Unitarian Association in Boston. "This little book," writes Eliot in his preamble, "Describes with accuracy the life of one of the to-be-forgotten millions." In truth, because of this "little book," which has never been long out of print, Gilley had taken his place in the pantheon of the to-be-forever-remembered.

The life Eliot describes is that of a frontier, pioneering man. Even surrounded by the bountiful resources of the sea — lobsters could be collected by hand along the shore in those days and fish were plentiful — getting by can only be described as an ordeal, especially in the winter months, when basic supplies ran low and a trip to Mount Desert Island could be impossible to undertake for weeks at a time on account of the weather.

Gilley, who settled on Sutton in 1854, brought great determination and ingenuity to eking out an island living; he had to be, in Eliot's words, "vigilant, patient, self-reliant, and brave" to make a go of it. He worked with what he had and could buy, farming and fishing as most of his neighbors did. Yet he took advantage of money-making opportunities as they arose, as when he started up a pogy-pressing factory during the Civil War, when the oil of this common fish became a sought-after commodity. The pogy chum made an excellent fertilizer for his crops.

In the late 1880s, Gilley showed even greater spirit and resolve. Well along in age, he began supplying fresh farm goods to summer cottages on the mainland, again taking advantage of the circumstances of the day, in this case the needs of the new people in the harbors. He rowed to Northeast and Southwest to deliver vegetables, milk and eggs, and brought back with him laundry, which his daughters washed and ironed.

It was on a return trip from Northeast Harbor to Sutton in 1896 that tragedy struck: Gilley's boat capsized and he drowned. "In half an hour," writes Eliot, "John Gilley had passed from a hearty and successful old age in this world, full of its legitimate interests and satisfactions, into the voiceless mystery of death." One wonders if it wasn't as much the particulars of Gilley's dying as his life that inspired the president of Harvard to write his biography.

It was in 1886, Eliot reports, that Gilley made his first sale of land "for summering purposes." The year after, and again in 1894, additional parcels were sold off, at prices that were "forty or fifty times any price which had ever been put on his [Gilley's] farm by the acre." Difficult to imagine, even in these inflated times, that an acre that once went for what was considered the astronomical price of $800 today may fetch as much as $350,000.

Gilley became a prosperous man, but in the process the land passed — irrevocably, for the most part — to summer people. As McLane has put it: "In the 1880s, Sutton Island underwent changes that eventually undermined the fabric of its social and economic life. Vacationers arrived." An era was coming to an end; from genealogies of families, Sutton Island's historical account would shift to genealogies of houses.

For example:

"[Isaac Richardson's] son William built a house for himself and wife, Nancy

Moore, in 1845, but at his early death in '66 it reverted to his father, who in '72 sold it to Leonard Holmes, who sold it in '87 to Orrin A. Donnell, who deeded it in '97 to his wife, Laura (daughter of John Gilley). They sold it in '08 to William Burnham, who gave it in '23 to his factotum, Leslie Bunker, who in '24 deeded it to his son Philip, who in '57 sold it to Eliza Fay Hawtin, the present owner and 9th possessor" (Paine, p. 6).

Besides attracting well-off individuals from East Coast cities, the island became something of an Ivy League outpost. Joshua Kendall, whom McLane describes as "the first rusticator to acquire a native homestead," deeded his home on the southeastern tip of Sutton to Harvard University, which continued to use it as a getaway for faculty. Likewise, Florence Hessenbruch deeded her house to Princeton; and Nelson Rockefeller bequeathed the "Tea House," built by Andrew C. Wheelwright on the north shore in 1895, to Ernest Martin Hopkins, president of Dartmouth College.

Many distinguished individuals visited or summered on Sutton, including John Burroughs, the early American naturalist. One of the most interesting steady summer visitors was Mary Cabot Wheelwright. Born in Boston in 1878, Wheelwright had a great passion for the religion and art of the American Indian and founded the Museum of Navajo Ceremonial Art in Santa Fe, New Mexico.

Sutton was Wheelwright's "part-time roost," as Louise Libby puts it. We get some sense of Sutton in her reminiscences, "Early Yachting Days at Northeast Harbor." There Wheelwright recounts the history of the FANNY EARL, a small coasting schooner built by Captain Eugene Stanley "in front of his house" on the southern shore of Sutton.

This vessel came to a sad end, as Wheelwright relates: "She was caught off Boon Island in December, in a gale, and all her sails were blown away. Captain Stanley had only one man with him and the vessel was loaded with sand. They drifted for many days, sometimes working her in to the coast a little way, but finally were picked up well out at sea, and taken to England, and as the steamers that rescued them wouldn't tow the FANNY EARL, which was still tight astray, Captain Stanley had to scuttle her and it nearly broke his heart. He got another vessel but was never well after the loss of his schooner and died within three years."

Such a disaster, when it happens to someone with means, can be shrugged off and a new venture started. But as Eliot wrote in his life of John Gilley, for New England islanders "the margin of livelihood" could be very close. "If the invest-

ments of the rich were as hazardous as are those of the poor," Eliot observed, "theirs would be a lot even more worrisome than it is now."

"The coming of the summer colonizers meant first the occupation of the northern shore and gradually of all but a few scattered homesteads on the south shore held by stubborn hangers-on," writes McLane. "Occupation" and "hangers-on" imply invasion and resistance. Whatever the actual circumstances, islanders moved off, some to the mainland, others to Great and Little Cranberry. By 1950, Sutton was, for all intents and purposes, a summer island.

Why did the island shift from a year-round community to a summer one? How is it that Sutton's situation did not allow it to continue to support fishermen and local industries as have the two

"The White Hen," the home of Mary C. Wheelwright on Sutton Island, ca. 1920. Photo courtesy of the Wheelwright Museum of the American Indian, Santa Fe, New Mexico.

Cranberries? Charles Rice states that his father moved his family from Sutton to Great Cranberry because there was more work there. Other native Sutton islanders married folk from Little and Great Cranberry and left to join their spouses.

Many year-rounders moved to Mt. Desert Island where there were greater resources, better public services and more opportunities to make a decent living. Abraham C. Fernald, who lived briefly on Sutton and who came the closest to establishing a viable business on the island, removed to Somesville and, according to McLane, ended his business career manufacturing caskets — "and one hopes it was not his ship-building career [on Sutton] that gave him the idea." (As Paine reported in 1963, A.C. Fernald's "two grandsons and great-grandson are still carrying on the Fernald store at Somesville.")

"Removed" is a favorite word of McLane's; in his account of Sutton, one individual after another "removes" to somewhere else, rarely to return to the island. In one case, a family was literally removed — posthumously. In 1924, the Gilley graveyard on Sutton was transferred to a family plot in Friendship, Maine. According to Ted Spurling, Sr., who corresponded with Earle Stanley, one of John Gilley's grandsons, summer people didn't

want to have the cemetery on their land and requested that it be moved.

Spurling feels that Sutton Island's lack of a decent harbor played a key role in the demise of the year-round settlement. At one point schooners were built on the island, yet the boatbuilding industry never took hold the way it did on Great and Little Cranberry, where it is carried on today.

There are few places on Sutton where vessels can be hauled up. And aside from a slight indentation at the southeastern end of the island, which is the most sheltered spot on its coastline, Sutton lies open to the full forces of nature. Many piers and floats have been destroyed by northeast gales and Atlantic hurricanes, and Paine tells of at least eight such shoreline structures that were "knocked to pieces by tempestuous seas."

Despite its relatively small size, which one would imagine might encourage the establishment of a close community, Suttons has always been a somewhat scattered colony, with people living independent of one another. There was a school for a time, which doubled as the Sutton Island public library; it closed in the 1920s, when the island lacked enough children to make it feasible, and was moved and converted into a summer home.

There never was a church on the island, except for a tiny chapel that a summer cottager, Reverend William B. Stimson, is said to have built behind his house (Reverend Paine also held summer services in the school house). The churches on Great and Little Cranberry have always been central gathering places for the islanders.

Electricity and phone service came late. Paine reports the stringing of electric power wires on the island in 1932. And there was nominal development of the roads, which, to this day, are no more than grassy thoroughfares.

"The chief reason the island failed as a year-round community," says Spurling, "is that the land and houses were bought up by summer people." This theory is seconded by Louise Libby: "People sold their property to summer people and moved off," she says. She blames some of the gentrification of the area on the real estate business, which tends to push the price of a property as high as it will go, with little thought to the effect such sales have on the stability of the year-round community. Libby sees this trend occurring today in Northeast Harbor, where many native year-rounders have opted to sell out and move away.

Many people consider Mattie Bunker, the postmistress, to have been the last native to leave Sutton. With her went the post office, which closed in 1947 — a final blow, in a certain sense, to the viability of a year-round community. A few non-natives lived through the winter after that. Most recently, Frederic and Elise Hawtin stayed on Sutton the year-round, but they were obliged to move to Northeast Harbor when Mr. Hawtin suffered a stroke five years ago.

Mrs. Hawtin notes that there never was an established community on Sutton. "It was grim living for those who tried to make a year-round home there," she states, and some natives, in her estimation, simply hated the island and couldn't wait to settle elsewhere.

Mrs. Hawtin mentions that her fellow summer islander, Mrs. Theodore Nussdorfer, who lives in New Hampshire, now presides over the Association for the Preservation of Sutton Island. She is in the process of gathering reminiscences from islanders about their homes and their histories. Mrs. Hawtin recognizes that Sutton has lost a community, but in her eye, "a new, informal community" has been established in its place, a seasonal one that cares deeply about the welfare of the island.

Schooner on the ways, Sutton Island, 1894

All five of the Cranberries have undergone change and continue to face demographic fluctuations and development issues in these times. Great Cranberry, for instance, has just begun the process of organizing a "Futures Group" to deal with issues of on-island and off-island schooling, tourism and harbor renovation. At the same time, a kind of "back to the future" enterprise has sprung up: following in the footsteps of John Gilley and other early islanders, Gary and Colleen Allen have started Cabin Creek Farm, supplying fresh produce and flowers to year-rounders and summerfolk.

From the Great Cranberry Island dock, Sutton Island forms a low-lying, smoky green-brown band beneath the distant, bare summits of Cadillac and Sargent. Circling the island you come upon old stone pilings, remnants of another time. At the southwestern tip there's a spit of shingle beach, Rice Point, that juts out in the water. Rounding the corner toward Bear Island you come upon a huge osprey nest perched on a tall rock outcrop. The spruce in the background are good-sized trees. They are the year-round residents now.

The late afternoon sun lights up the side of the houses along the southern shore, their rough-cut lawns descending to the tide line. Some houses are nestled in the woods, others stand out, their owners having carved out sizable yards from the surrounding trees.

These are the houses Admiral Morison so admired. "Now we close-haul the sails again to pass between Suttons Island and the two Cranberries," he wrote in an essay, "An August Day's Sail" (1963).

I turn my back on the Islesford shore where the summer houses are pretentiously inappropriate, but linger lovingly on the south shore of Sutton, its little cottages built in the simple taste of a century ago, when Maine men knew how to create a house as beautiful as a ship. . . Sutton, with its memories of John Gilley and Mary Wheelwright, of picnics long ago, of clumps of blue harebell growing like weeds from the wild grass.

By contrast, George Paine's final words on Sutton Island come off sounding showman-like: "If you take the sage advice of the grand man who led Harvard for 40 thrilling years (1869-1909) you will make your way to this land of pure delight, Sutton Island, Maine."

And then there is the more poetic conclusion of Dorothy Simpson, island author: "So the Cranberry Isles are New World cousins to all the isles of history and mythology: the Spice Islands, the Fortunate Isles, the isles of Greece, and Vachel Lindsay's 'wizard islands, of august surprise.'"

Like those Old World isles, the Cranberries float, mirage-like, on their granite moorings. Sutton seems the most mysterious of them all, private, untrammeled, an island outside of time.

Carl Little is the author of Paintings of Maine, Edward Hopper's New England *and, forthcoming,* Winslow Homer and the Sea.

"The island has changed some, but not too much."

Charles Rice was born on Sutton on January 15, 1904. "That makes me 39," he says with a chuckle. His father was a carpenter and built boats and houses. Rice lives with his wife, Ada, on Dog Point Road, about midway down the length of Great Cranberry.

Rice recalls that in the early days Sutton Island was divided pretty evenly between natives and summer people, the former on the southern shore, the latter on the northern. There was no church; when asked where the family attended church, he replies, "We didn't go." He remembers that islanders routinely rowed to other islands as well as to Northeast and Southwest Harbors. One man, he says, used to row to Mt. Desert Rock, 20 miles out to sea, to visit his girlfriend.

Rice had an uncle on Sutton who had cows and hens, and kept a small garden, which others had as well. He remembers delivering milk in the pitch dark, with only the faintest dawn light visible through the spruce. He had an aunt, Mattie Bunker, who ran the post office. "She may have been the last of the natives to stay on Sutton's," he says.

Rice went to New York as a young man to live with a brother. He lived near Van Cortland Park and worked for the *Bronx Home News.* From there he went to grade school in Braintree, Massachusetts, and worked as a plumber. When he came back to Maine, he captained boats. He recalls sailing a 64-foot yacht, the LEGLONG, back and forth between the Cranberries and Philadelphia. The vessel belonged to the Robinettes, who had a summer place in Northeast Harbor.

For many years, Rice ran a boat for Joshua Kendall, an architect with the firm McKim, Mead and White in New York City. Kendall had a summer home at the eastern end of Sutton. Rice remembers Kendall saying once, "When I die, I don't want to go to heaven or hell. I want to go to Purgatory. That's where all the women are."

Physically, Rice says, Sutton has changed some, "but not too much." He and his wife remember there being more open spaces, more wildflowers and blueberries.

As the interview nears its end, Rice shares a memory of a hurricane that once struck the islands. "The winds were so strong," he relates, "that some hens were blown from Cranberry all the way over to Sutton's."

Charles Rice in the 1930s

Fine days, hunter's moons

From Islesford, Capt. Ted Spurling, Sr., chronicles day-to-day life

*S*ince 1993, Captain Ted Spurling, Sr., has delighted Inter-Island News *readers with his seasonal reporting of events on the Cranberry Islands from his perch at the center of the universe, Islesford, Maine. Descended from one of Islesford's founding families, in his long and varied career as fisherman, seaman, local historian and writer, Captain Ted has combined the intricate sensitivity of the native-born islander to weather, tide, and the rhythm of local life, with a global — and occasionally deeply philosophical — perspective that make his columns always fresh, sometimes surprising.* Island Journal *is pleased to recap a year of the high points of these columns. Certainly they create a fascinating vignette of an island community, at work and at play, throughout the year.*

Winter '94 — a deep freeze to remember!

This has been an extra-rugged winter, but looking back through some written records and talking with a few of our older citizens who remembered, it could be considered rather mild when compared with the winter of 1923.

That year, two large coal vessels came ashore on the Cranberry Islands, spilling out their cargoes of coal. On January 12, 1923, the three-master DON PARSONS struck on Bar Beach near the Coast Guard station at 4:15 a.m. The next day, on Old Point on Great Cranberry Island, another three-master, the GENERAL JOHN HOGG, was also wrecked, there still being strong easterly winds with snow and vapor flying. Luckily, all from both vessels were saved. The crew was taken off the latter vessel by U.S. Coast Guard men at about 9:30 a.m.

This report of the winter of early 1923 was taken from Andrew Stanley's Islesford diary:

On Feb. 17, *the harbor here was pretty well frozen over, as far as you could see, and well up towards Southwest Harbor (approximately 3.5 miles away).*

On Feb. 19, *a gang of men attempted to walk the ice to Southwest Harbor, hauling a skiff along on a sled as a precaution, with each man carrying a long, light pole in case he broke through. Then the pole could be stretched across the ice to hold him up until rescued. They made the journey safely and returned. Some of the men also walked over to Northeast Harbor, about the same distance from Little Cranberry.*

Feb. 24. *As the cold weather and ice continued, five gangs walked again to Southwest Harbor for supplies.*

March 1, 1923. *Most of the ice broke up during the night and went out with the tide. Clarence Spurling and Will Spurling went out to haul their lobster traps — the first time since Feb. 12 — the lobster price being way up to 60 cents per pound.*

Now a return to this past winter, which compared to 1923, does not sound too bad. We have had more ice around the docks, also over in the "crick" at Great Cranberry, and at Northeast Harbor, than for several years.

Life and work goes on as usual. The coldest day here was on January 26, when the thermometer read 8 degrees below zero at 6 a.m.

Terry Johnson, our fuel oil man, gives us good service. The oil is barged over from Mount Desert Island to fill Terry's fuel tanks here; and his red island oil truck then takes it to the houses. Many of the islanders burn wood, and much of that is barged on also.

Jan. 29. A beautiful day and the temperature is way up at 40 degrees Fahrenheit.

Feb. 2, Groundhog Day. "When he looked around, his shadow he found. . ." Some lobster fishermen, scallopers and urchin boats are out. Our Islesford library is open on Tuesdays and Thursdays. Cindy Thomas is our librarian. The school children use its facilities a great deal. The school has also put out a newspaper titled *Islesford Globe*. School news, island news, fiction and non-fiction, poems and drawings are contributed by the students.

Feb. 11. Five degrees below zero at 6 a.m. and a hazy ring around the sun. A school party today for the school children of the primary room.

Feb. 16. Wind NE, temp. 30 degrees. Fog whistle moaning out east, and snow.

Feb. 17. A fine clear day with wind NW. The new fallen snow is clean and sparkling — like a freshly frosted cake. Some people are out cross-country (or rather, cross-island) skiing.

March 3. NE snow storm. The afternoon ferry boat run was canceled. Poor visibility, winds gusting to 60 miles per hour, rough seas and the glass reading has dropped to 28.86.

March 7. Town Meeting day. A goodly attendance. It went off fairly smoothly. Not like some that I have witnessed in the past. A fine lunch was held at the Neighborhood House at noontime. Annette Naegel of the Island Institute attended the meeting. So did Bud Dwelley, president of our historical society, who made a special trip here for a few days to attend the meeting.

March 14. Many fish boats out today and some of the men are bringing in traps. Lobsters are up to $4.75 per pound, but the yield is very low. Bruce Fernald and Jack Merrill, in their large, able lobster boats DOUBLE TROUBLE and BOTTOM DOLLAR, are taking out and standing by for sea urchin divers.

Quite a bit of this new fishing enterprise is going on in our area, with ample unloading of this prickly commodity at Northeast Harbor.

Sunday, March 20. Spring arrived at 3:28 p.m. in the northern hemisphere. A fair day it was, with the temperature at 35 degrees and a NW wind.

March 24. Rickey Alley, an Islesford lobster fisherman and artist, has won third place in the New Hampshire duck stamp contest, with honorable mention in the Maine contest. In 1988 Rick came in first in the duck stamp contest in Maine.

"Life and work goes on as usual. The coldest day here was on January 26, when the thermometer read 8 degrees below zero at 6 a.m."

June 29.
Thick o'fog all day and a few rain showers. The deer are plentiful and enjoying our gardens.

March 27. Wind south on this day — temperature 38 degrees F — overcast and rain, later changing to snow. March came in like a frisky lamb and went out likewise, on a sunny, windy day.

April 1. We could see and hear a large flock of wild geese winging their way north this morning. Our newly installed orange street lights give an eerie glow, when looking out the windows at night. And on awakening in a dark house, it looks like something is afire.

April 3 (Sunday). A nice Easter service. Lobstermen are busy rigging their traps for the hoped-for spring spurt. Wind and rain storm tonight.

April 18. Two funerals recently. Both burials at our Sand Beach cemetery. Ida Spurling, aged 95. A longtime neighbor and friend. And Katrina Pickering, aged 19, who died in an auto accident. A very sudden and sad event. Ida's committal on April 8 and Katrina's the 16th. A beautiful lone heron had been seen recently in a pond in back of this peaceful little spot.

April 20. An annual meeting of the Cranberry Island Fisherman's Co-op at the Neighborhood House at 3 p.m. On the board of directors are: Roy Hadlock, Lyn Colby, Paul Thormann, Bruce Fernald and James Bright. James Bright is president and Ted Spurling Jr. is the clerk. They voted for and will buy a one-ton Chevrolet truck with an insulated12-by-8-by-8-foot box on back, for hauling lobsters to various off-island customers. They may also use this vehicle for lobster bait later, if necessary. Right now bait has been easier to get than in previous springs.

April 22. Temperature 42 degrees, wind south by west. Some sun, some rain and a snow squall. I have been helping Carol Hall of Southwest Harbor prepare a list of the known men of this area who were drowned or lost at sea. There will be a monument erected in their memory soon, at Manset.

April 25. A full pink moon tonight. Also at perigee. This "in line" position of the moon and sun causes extra high and low tides. Good clamming tides, if you can find any clams. What a good job we have done in just about totally depleting most all of our fisheries. I remember my boyhood days in the 1930s, trawling and handlining for ample catches of haddock and codfish with my father. You could catch flounders (for a three-day lobster trap baiting), off the bottom at low tide, at the mouth of the "crick" at Great Cranberry Island. Sad it is indeed to realize that those days are no more. Dave Mills of our Southwest Harbor Oceanarium has sent me a leaflet on "loons and lobsters."

April 30. Temperature 58 degrees, wind north, a fuzzy-looking sun. Six deer browsing on Warren Ferland's lawn, this early morn. Rebecca Albright, the music teacher from Otis, Maine, came over to give lessons to some of the island "small fry" today. A quick grass fire flared up at the town gravel pit. Some folks tried to beat it out, with little success. Cory Alley got out our fire truck to the rescue and the fire was quickly quenched.

May 4. Lobsters are down in price. Right now, to $2.50 per pound. This has caused many of our lobstermen to get their lobster cars ready for launching. They will store their catches for better times. NE winds to 40 knots. Rough seas outside.

May 19. Islesford school children went off to Frenchboro (on Outer Long Island) on the Island Institute's good boat RAVEN. They will return tomorrow. Richard and Sue Hill are back from their auto trip to the Panama Canal Zone. They are getting some of the stored boats from their boatyard here ready for launching. Sue will be getting her gift shop, "Winter's Work," ready at the Islesford Restaurant Dock, in a little while. Marion Baker's pottery shop will be opening there for another season.

Sunday, May 22. A fine and noble day. Most lobster boats out. The Islesford Museum had an open house today — noon to 4:15 p.m. Debbie Wade and Fred Pardy, park officials, were present. People came from off-island too. Refreshments were served out under the trees. Gale Grandgent, vice president of our historical society, presiding over refreshments. Louise Libby, our former museum curator and daughter of Professor Sawtelle, our museum's founder and first curator, was present. The museum's artifacts are newly arranged in an attractive manner and the inside lighting is changed and improved. Work has been going on at the nearby restaurant dock as well and the floats are rigged and waiting. They plan to open officially on June 11.

May 23. Temperature 60 degrees, wind SE, sunny. Al Silverman and his lawn-mowing crew arrived on the morning mail boat. They mowed, clipped and raked at many homes and at two of our cemeteries. Johnny Moran is out and busy also with his riding mower, trailer cart and accessories. The school children are off and away again—this time to climb a mountain. The full flower moon will be in partial eclipse tomorrow evening. This follows the eclipse of the sun on May 10.

May 27. Roy Hadlock got a halibut this morning at about 7 a.m. It was caught about a quarter of a mile east of the whistle buoy off Baker's Island. He mentioned it over his boat radio and quickly had orders for some of it. So it was pretty nigh all sold out before he even fetched port. It was caught on just one trawl of 80 hooks on a 24-hour set. The other baited hooks yielded a few small sculpin and nothing more. This is the first halibut caught near here this spring. It weighed out at 38 pounds. "Me and the Mrs." had a goodly portion of it for our supper. And as the old-timers used to say, "It was some old good!"

May 30. Memorial Day started out with rain and fog. The island school children with others and adults walked to the graves of our island cemeteries and placed evergreen boughs and flags on the veterans' graves. Also singing appropriate hymns and reciting the Lord's Prayer at each site. On June 6 there will be two students graduating from the Islesford Grammar School, Jeremy Alley and Brandon Russell.

Ah, summer!

June 21 (Tuesday). Summer has arrived . . . it came in at 10:48 a.m.

A gray morning with intermittent sunshine. We are also on our summer ferry boat schedule. More boats and more people. Selig Harrison was on the TV news tonight, discussing problems concerning North Korea. Sig and his wife, Barbara, own a summer home just down the road "a ways" from us.

June 23. A full strawberry moon tonight and extra high and low tides again. Some of the men have been carring up their lobsters for a while, as the price had taken a sickening plunge. It has started to go up again, as it usually does just before the 4th of July. So those who carred will make a fair profit. A trip off-island today to have another starter put on the mainland car. Hope this holds out better than the last three . . . a good old car in most ways but she has never been too partial to her starters.

June 29. Thick o'fog all day and a few rain showers. The deer are plentiful and enjoying our gardens.

July 4. A fine clear morning with a thin, waning crescent moon. Aunt Cindy's tea roses are in full bloom, looking like puffy white snow balls on their bushes out back.

"March came in like a frisky lamb and went out likewise, on a sunny, windy day."

A noon picnic for all hands today at the town field. A few soft shell lobsters are beginning to show up in some of the catches and a few tinker mackerel are being jigged in places. A very nice sunset this evening.

George Shirey has loaned a fine model of the steamboat J.T. MORSE to the museum. It is on display there. Well do I remember this handsome white paddle wheel steamboat and my boyhood trips on her with my family around the hills of Mt. Desert. Putting into Northeast, Seal and Bar Harbors. And occasionally to Rockland to connect with the Boston boat. I was nine years old when she made her last run in these waters. A pretty sight, also, to see her trim white hull showing sharp against the dark green background of the islands. Her steam whistle, similar to that of the old-time locomotives, gave a truly romantic setting to a pretty summer's scene.

July 10 (Sunday). "Rain before seven" and it cleared before "'leven." We need more rain. Our little dug wells are getting low. The fog burned off by mid morning. A "July Maypole" was erected in our town field this p.m. and many of the island folk, their friends and visitors danced around it, winding its various colored ribbons into different weaves and patterns. This is the third consecutive year in recent times of this interesting and merry event. Sally Corson and Dick Atlee are its sponsors. Many, many years ago, as I guess I once mentioned, a Maypole was put up on Little Cranberry Island near the point, which still bears that name. This custom,

according to history and legend, was begun by a beautiful French lady, Marguerite (LaCroix) Stanley, the wife of John. They were our first permanent settlers.

July 16. The Cranberry Island Lobster Co-op is in full operation and going strong, with its manager Peter Jones, assistant Chris Costello, and bookkeeper Frances Bartlett. The price of lobsters right now is thus: hard shells, $4 per pound; jumbo hards, $4.50; soft shell (shedders) $2.50 per. Warren Fernald is selling off his old wooden traps to the island visitors. These old "originals" are rapidly becoming collector's items.

A fine clear evening. Venus is flashing brightly in the WNW and Jupiter, too, shines brightly, but more to the SW, with the waxing moon nearby. Fragments of the predicted renegade comet are soon to begin slamming into Jupiter, they tell us. A bit scary to realize, especially as it is a planet in our own solar system and figuring the vastness of space . . . . Just next door, so to speak. . . .

July 20. Foggy early, then sunny and hot all day. Wind SW and the fog is still outside. Although July is usually the foggiest month in these parts, this year it seems to be more so than usual. I heard an-old timer a few years ago tell one of our transient touristers about how thick it was once, years ago, when he was shingling his barn. "Why," he said, "before I realized it, after I had gotten to the edge of the roof, I had shingled about eight feet out into that there fog!" Then seeing the look of disbelief on her face, he modified it a bit by quickly adding "but it was fairly easy a'drawing out the nails from the fog, when I realized my mistake."

And so quickly back to fall. . .

The summer season with its various activities, swarms of touristers and boating trips at all hours, has "came and went," as an old island neighbor once declared.

Aug. 22. A good steady rain last night. This will help the island wells. Ours got down to 17 inches a while back but today, when I sounded it, it read 24 inches. Our little dug well has never failed us yet. Many of our neighbors have drilled wells. But a couple of those nearby had to have their intake pipes extended a few years ago. They say now that the only water we get is just that from rainfall on the island and not, as was believed by many of us, supplemented by water filtering in under the sea floor from the larger land mass of Mount Desert and the mainland. A large, lovely rainbow was seen after this welcomed rainfall.

Aug. 30. Fine and clear. Wind west to 20 knots. A lot of people walking the roads today. Quite a few bicycles here also.

Brought on by the ferry boats. We spotted a bicycle built for two, several times this summer. The last time I rode one of those was with a friend in Central Park, New York, back in World War II days. The Sand Beach Road is a popular walk and riding strip. Richard Hill has been busy lately hauling up and storing boats for the winter at his yard there. On one of the Frank Newlin boat houses is a sign — "Ben Dover Boat Yard." A most appropriate play on words. A friend, Wayne Beal, who now lives in California, was telling me about his boat, the WATER LILY, named from his wife, Lily. Walter Hadlock, who once lived here, had a son Russell. He figured a good name for his new boat would be WALRUS.

Monday, Sept. 5. Labor Day. Overcast and windy. "Rain before seven" and it didn't clear before 'leven . . . a Northeast storm, winds getting up to 60 knots later. Rough seas outside. A bridge and float of a summer cottage facing our Eastern Way broke loose and were demolished. Roy Hadlock's lobster car broke loose and drifted off, but he found it later, over across on Great Cranberry, and fetched it back. Electrical power went out on the eastern end of our island but stayed on the western end. A lot of people braved the elements and did go to the Dock Restaurant for its last meal of the season. This part of Little Cranberry kept its electricity. The very active and pleasant summer season that was enjoyed by so many is coming to an end. Summer families leaving daily on the boats.

Sept. 6. School started today. A new teacher, Janet Fader, for the grammar room is replacing Steve Korman, who is taking a stint at lobster fishing for a while — easing into this contrasting vocation as sternman aboard Ted Jr.'s boat PANDORA. Rob Mocarsky will be teaching again in the primary room. The same number of students this year as last. The two boys who graduated were replaced by two little beginners, Emily Thomas and Jamie Thormann.

We went on the off-season ferry boat schedule today, which will be followed by the winter one on October 24. The Islesford Museum also has changed its schedule to Tuesday through Saturday only, and will close September 30.

Sept. 27. Sunny all morning but wind NE. The SUNBEAM over today for an island funeral. William E. Hadlock, the last of his generation, was brought over on the Sea Coast Mission boat with family and friends. Rev. Ted Hoskins (of the mission staff) officiated at the service, at our Congregational church. Bill was laid to rest in the old Hadlock-Stanley cemetery. He descends from both of these early island families.

Oct. 10. Today is Columbus Day. I wonder what the Admiral of the Ocean Sea would think of our Western Hemisphere, right now. Were he able to come see and hear it for a while — possibly he might wonder if maybe he should have held off a bit? Although he wasn't the first to discover it, at least one can say when he did, it stayed discovered.

Oct. 12. Wednesday, a mite colder, 35 degrees at 5 a.m., and wind is north. Sent for my lobster license today. Half price (for me now) as it's after October. So the application form says; some advantages to being older, I suppose. A few touristers wandering about.

Oct. 14. Another nice day. Hazy early and a light wind. We were supposed to have flu shots yesterday, to be given at the Neighborhood House. Sponsored "free gratootis" by our town. The needle nurse embarked from Northeast Harbor, but on stopping first at Great Cranberry Island (from the ferry) she checked her needles and found them all to be the wrong kind and too short. "Anyway," she informed us afterwards, "I had a good boat ride, and I shall return."

Oct. 17. Terry Johnson has made his rounds recently and filled many of our island home fuel tanks to start out the winter. This morning he barged off Phil and Molly Bowditch in their little island auto. They pack it with their summer belongings and are barged over with it in the early summer. They use this car on the island, while here, at their summer cottage. Then come fall, are barged off again with all their things needed inside, and drive back to their winter home in Massachusetts. A very practical way to do it. Saves a lot of handling. They call the car their "summer suitcase."

Oct. 19. A nice Indian summer day. Some large lush rose hips on the bushes at the sand beach. Loaded with Vitamin C. The only complaint: I wish they were seedless. The beach spinach and tiny beach peas are very tasty, too, when in season, although it takes a lot of picking to get a fair mess.

A friend recently gave us some fennel plants from his garden. They have a stimulating, sweet smell. It brings to mind the paregoric and hot water Mother used to give me to combat an earache, when I was a boy, and I would drop off into a blissful, sound sleep. Many old home remedies were given then. Spirits of nitre, for stomach soothing — and Dr. True's Elixir (supposed to be good for anything) and the asthamador powder that we used to light up in a saucer and inhale its smoke for a relief from asthma and hay fever. And it worked! But many of the old remedies are sold no longer. I used to say to friends occasionally, in Mother's hearing, "Yup, I was raised on paregoric" — just to hear her indignant "You were not!" For she was always cautious and moderate with these older remedies. No sulfur and molasses, though such was used earlier.

A full hunter's moon tonight.

Oct. 22. Saturday and wind NE. A goodly amount of rain yesterday. But it slacked off today. Plenty of water in the ground. Most welcomed for our wells. The cellar sump pump barely keeping up at times. Rough seas a'roaring outside.

Oct. 25. Temp. 55, waning moon and stars showing early. Then foggy. We're on the winter ferry boat schedule.

The lobster fishing has been fine this season, with good hauls and the price better than last year. It stayed around $2.40 per pound for some time, once reaching up to $2.50 per. It has started now to go down and some of the men are preparing their lobster cars and might store their catches for a while if it continues. Right now it is down to $2.10.

The nurse for the flu shots came today and they were given. Starting at 1 p.m. (for all who wished to have one). Quite a few came. Nurse Norella Pittle officiated.

Oct. 31. Sunny early but a weather change later and a raw SE wind by nightfall and barometer dropping fast and rain. But the school children and little ones were out and about tonight in their Halloween masks and costumes for the customary "trick or treat." Our change to Eastern Standard Time has made it get dark earlier. There were also some tricks instead of treats amongst our lobstermen. One of them discovered his pickup trick to be tampered with in the tire department and another found his rowboat dangling on high from a tree limb.

Nov. 3. Clear morning. Stars shine bright at 5 a.m. Also we are having high run tides, there being a new moon at perigee. Wind NE to 30 knots early, then dropped out as the tide turned ebb. Most lobster boats fishing. Several lobstermen getting their lobster cars ready, as the price is low. The Coast Guard over to the co-op dock today to check and inspect the facilities for receiving, storing and handling the fuel oil here. (A tanker delivers it to us.) All is OK.

Nov. 7. NW wind today, gale force with gusts over 60 knots. All lobster boats on moorings, but our good old mail boat ferry made its runs. A meeting was held tonight at the Mount Desert Regional High School at 7 p.m. The school board members there voted on whether to continue accepting tuition students from surrounding towns, including the Cranberry Isles. On a six to four vote in favor, they decided to continue. But the members will seek an amendment to the state law limiting the rate paid.

Nov. 9. And now Election Day "has come and went" and we can hope for a return to "normalcy." Some of us are pleased with the results, some maybe not. But many of us agree, I think, that a shake-up and a change were necessary. We will miss all the signs and posters on the highways and byways, as we zip along! Down at our Town Dock one lone one, however, does remain. It reads: "Vote for Tom Alley for Governor. The 'Green Stuff' Party Candidate."

We hope everyone had a nice Thanksgiving, and a very merry Christmas to you all.

"The Ocean Is Our Common Birthplace"

(continued from page 11)

Compared with other waters, the Gulf of Maine appears to be one of the more pristine bodies of water in the world. But we should not wait until damage occurs before we act. And we have plenty of advance warning of potential damage.

Scientific studies indicate that the gulf may be threatened by a number of toxic pollutants and has already been affected by habitat loss.

Unnaturally high levels of toxins in the gulf's deep basin sediments indicate that these contaminants are distributed throughout the gulf system. PCBs and heavy metals have appeared in the tomalley of lobsters caught near Boston Harbor. Recently, unnaturally high levels of dioxins were found in the tomalley of lobsters taken from areas off the Maine coast.

Clam harvests in Downeast Maine declined from 4.6 million pounds in 1982 to 500,000 pounds in 1993. Over a third of the gulf's shellfish beds are closed because of bacterial contamination at any given time.

Development of coastal lands has destroyed habitat critical for waterfowl, migratory birds and other wildlife, including commercially harvested fish.

The Gulf of Maine is a microcosm that mirrors in smaller detail most of the problems reflected in the wide world's experience of oceanic degradation.

We should not wait until the seas off our coasts are as filthy as the Mediterranean or as toxic as the Sea of Azov before we take steps to monitor and correct the problems. We should not be lured by superficial geographical differences into the belief that because the gulf isn't an inland sea, it can't be seriously contaminated. We know it can be. We should make sure it won't be. The way to do that is to act, not to wait.

What's needed is an approach that crosses manmade political boundaries to bring together the needs the gulf serves for the communities that live along its shores.

The most important role government can play is, in some ways, a role difficult for government to play.

That is a role that allows citizens to manage the resources to which their lives are linked.

Government cannot solve environmental problems in a vacuum. Laws like the Clean Water Act and the Clean Air Act have removed great amounts of pollution from our environment, but in the end it is the choices made by communities and individuals that are responsible for the long-term health of our environment.

"We should be listening . . . to the experience of those who work the fishery."

Peter Ralston

THE HUMAN FACTOR

When the challenges are as complex as the ones the Gulf of Maine communities face, it's even more important for citizens to take part in finding solutions.

Mainers have been working our seas for generations. Children have learned from parents about the seas and the fish. We ought to be using and analyzing this practical knowledge, not asking those who have it to stand to one side while the experts take charge.

The collapse of the New England fishery isn't a local phenomenon. It reflects a worldwide phenomenon, one whose full effects are becoming apparent only now.

We ought to be sharing with our fishermen the predictive abilities science has given us about sustainable fisheries. But we should be listening as well to the experience of those who work the fishery.

I am told that "anecdotal" information isn't scientifically useful. I respond, with all respect, that when our overall scientific understanding is as thinly based as our knowledge of the oceans is today, a more appropriate stance would be to say that all information is potentially useful.

The value of human knowledge rests in the use human beings can make of it. Scientific management of our fishery that leaves out the people whose lives depend upon it isn't scientific. It's arrogant and it's going to fail. Other nations have taken advantage of the knowledge of those who work their fisheries. It is time we learned to do so here, as well.

It is my vision that we should seek a Gulf of Maine environment that is naturally healthy, sustainable and one from which people can make a livelihood.

I believe in an environment that includes the work and existence of human beings. I believe human beings and their demands are as potentially sympathetic to the environment as the demands of nesting falcons or spawning salmon.

I also believe that it is a goal that cannot be met through government study and regulation alone. Saving the Gulf of Maine, the oceans, the lives of those who inhabit the coastal regions of our nations is going to require a concerted effort on the part of all people. Public-private partnerships are going to be a critical factor in our success or failure.

Organizations such as the Island Institute have an important role to play. You have an ability to reach out to people, to educate, to encourage, to brainstorm. I applaud the efforts you have already made, and implore you to keep at it.

Lord Byron, the English poet, wrote 200 years ago, "Roll on thou deep and dark blue oceans, roll, ten thousand fleets sweep over thee in vain, Man marks the earth with ruin — his control stops with the shore. . . ."

Those words capture the magic and mystery of the oceans for humankind. It's the magic and mystery fishermen know and part of what binds them to their lives on the sea. It's part of what everyone in Maine feels about the oceans and it is, in a larger sense, part of what the whole human family knows to be true.

The ocean is our common birthplace. It has its large share of human tragedies and pain and mistakes. But is has always stood for something larger than mankind, something more enduring and more permanent. It is our responsibility to keep that symbol clean for our children and theirs.

George Mitchell represented Maine in the Senate for nearly 15 years, and retired as Senate Majority Leader in 1995.

Eye of the RAVEN

(continued from page 7)

But onward. We know that Sears Island is a no-win debate as it stares out at us from the hollow-eyed shores of Waldo County, where decades of rural poverty have exacted their grim toll. Tomorrow in Castine, a panel of opponents and proponents will state their cases to the 225 people who will attend the Island Conference. Where is Penobscot Bay and its islands' future headed, and what role will Sears Island and Mack Point (and we) play in this future?

Making her way back out into deeper water, RAVEN heads north past Stockton Springs to Sandy Point, where the bay narrows again and the tide and currents begin dancing in more complex syncopations. Massive sand deposits line the shores, past which glacial rivers once roared. The chart shows a large expanse of 'sft' on the bottom, denoting the gravel deposits left by these same raging rivers. It is here, old-time bay fishermen will tell you, on these gravel bottoms where river and bay waters mix, that cod used to come in large numbers to spawn. Only 50 years gone. Little patches of foam float mysteriously by, like some unearthly flotilla of by-the-wind sailors, the first reminder that the Penobscot is also a major industrial artery.

Just to the north of Gundalow Cove, the tidal current noticeably increases as the lunar surge from the bay collides head-on with the force of the river that drains a massive watershed to the north. In the main channel of the river between Verona Island and the basaltic cliffs of Bucksport, the Penobscot hurries by the green cans that mark the deep water; a few remaining lobster trap buoys stream away in the current, which runs by us at greater than five knots.

Here also in the coolness of the morning, a thick valley fog has formed, giving an eerie sensation on the water; we can hear traffic on the suspension bridge at Bucksport, but we cannot see the bridge until we are underneath, staring up at its girders. The radar goes on as we glide past the shores of the bay's only mill town, busy noises from which can be heard through the gauzy opacity. Moments later, out of the top of the fog, the stack of Champion International appears, and we can just make out the pier where we will stop on our way back downstream.

We're another two miles upriver when the sun finally burns through the fog, and reveals a wondrous Indian summer day. We glide over the smooth black waters of the river past Prospect, Frankfort and Winterport. Just above Buck Point we interrupt a doe crossing the river, the current sweeping her down across our bow, startled to be caught changing shores and browsing grounds.

Above and below us for virtually the entire length of the river north of Bucksport, the shores are lined with tawny marsh grasses, a fringing salt marsh complex that collectively adds a significant amount of nutrient enrichment to these waters. We begin to see evidence of waterfowl; first in twos and threes and then in

Island Institute Schools Director Jim Wilmerding (left) visited the Frenchboro school aboard RAVEN in January. With Jim are (front row) teacher Heather Hurlburt, Zack Lunt, Luke Higgins, teacher's aide April Wiggins and Travis Lunt; (back row) Nate Lunt, Kristi Lunt, Chuck Redmond and Joseph Lunt.

larger numbers of winged shadows that start up from the grasses and shallows and careen off to port and starboard. Behind the salt marshes are extensive stands of white pine set off amid the splendid coloration of mixed northern hardwoods. There are remarkably few houses visible from the water; in fact, we're completely captured by the variety and integrity of the landscape and sore amazed we've never been here before. At Crosby Narrows, perhaps the single grandest spot on this astonishing run of river, the millennial work of the Penobscot has carved a narrow deep trench through the highlands, and soaring overhead is a lone, totemic eagle.

Too soon we are past Hampden Highlands, but Bangor heaves into view at a turn in the river. We plan to tie up at the city wharf, but can't resist poking up under the pair of bridges that connect Bangor and Brewer, beyond the chart datum, edging up into the Bangor Pool below the dam. The tide, which was low in Rockland at 5:45 a.m., has just begun to turn here at 11 a.m. Slowly, slowly, for this is no man's land for RAVEN. And then on the far shore out of a large pine a pair of adult bald eagles rises and soars and soon resettles in a nearby tree, unconcerned by our presence. Here is a little piece of Maine's timelessness reflected in the still waters of the Pool. A few people framed in the high-rise windows of Eastern Maine Medical Center tentatively wave, and then

someone grabs a pillow case and begins wildly waving it — an ensign, signifying . . . something. These eagles make our day, too.

Alongside the city pier, we fall into conversation with the harbormaster, who is un-rigging the floats at the end of his season. "It's been a long while since I' seen a boat your size go up in there. Of course it's nothing but a rockpile, but you probably knew that." The harbormaster says more boats than ever before made the trip up the Penobscot and tied up at the city marina this year, and he's hopeful that more will continue to come, infusing the water's edge with a remnant of Bangor's glorious days of shipping that ended half a century ago and still give a lonely and unused air to the scene.

After lunch we catch the ebbing tide and begin retracing our course. On the way downstream we have enough time and just enough tide to poke into Marsh Cove, the huge salt marsh below Frankfort that is perhaps the single most ecologically significant feature of the lower river. It is replete, as it should be, with the black silhouettes of nervous waterfowl.

At around 3:00 in the afternoon, we pull into the cove below the Champion International mill where once massive booms of pulpwood rose and fell on the tides when the wood that supplied the mill came in over the water by tug and barge. We are met by Bill Grady, who has offered to take us through the mill. With hard hats and safety glasses we climb the narrow stairs to the four-story wood room, where four-foot bolts of spruce and fir tumble off the conveyor and are fed into the jaws of huge granite grinders. Champion still relies on this "groundwood" process to grind up wood fibers, rather than supposedly more modern pulping processes that break down fibers chemically. As a result, Champion's waste stream is significantly more benign.

We descend from the wood room and walk out onto the floor of the mill where the enormous paper machines spew forth a fine stream of wood pulp on wool felts that absorb some of the water, leaving the remainder to be taken out by steam heat down the way. At a certain point on the production line, you can point to where liquid pulp becomes dry paper while the line roars by at 3,200 feet per minute (about 35 miles an hour) to produce 1,250 tons of paper per day. At the end of the line, high-quality, lightweight coated paper is collected on enormous rolls that are cut and packaged and sent to the shipping depot.

Bill tells us that the last few years of

recession and decreased advertising revenues for magazines have battered pulp and paper companies across the globe, but Champion has actually increased its market share in the competitive world of lightweight coated papers. Twenty-four out of 25 of the top-selling magazines in the country are printed on paper from this mill. Champion's strategy has been built in part on the recognition that the customers of their customers, magazine readers of such American mainstays as *Time, Newsweek, Cosmopolitan, Family Circle* and *Ladies Home Journal* (and *Island Journal*) demand an environmentally friendly product, meaning "elementally" chlorine-free paper, with a high recycled content. "We're at the forefront of environmental commitment in the paper industry," says Bill. "It's a commitment that comes from the top and it is very, very important to the company because we think it gives us a competitive edge."

At their large waste water treatment plant, which handles 13 million gallons of treated effluent per day, I am struck by the dense sweet growths of moss and duckweed growing in the clarifying tanks. The treatment here is based on a phosphoric acid and anhydrous ammonia process for settling out solids (the sludge from which is burned, along with tire chips, waste wood and coal in the mill's power plant) rather than on the processes one finds at municipal treatment plants that rely significantly on chlorine for purification. I ask about Champion's chlorine use, chlorine being the single most toxic chemical to marine life when it enters saltwater. Bill points out that neither their bleaching process nor their waste water treatment process rely on chlorine; but they do use 660 gallons of chlorine per day for treating their freshwater intake to kill off algae and other life which could interfere with their manufacturing process. So, there appears to be at least some room for improvement, and it's good to know that this industrialial giant takes the challenge seriously.

We return to RAVEN, fire her up and take one last circumnavigation of Champion's waterfront, past an outfall pipe that bubbles up from below, past the NETEPENEWESIT, the state's emergency oil spill barge, which is berthed here, back out into the main channel of the river, where a rising wind and tide tug away at a lonely lobster pot buoy waving in the current.

Castine beckons not far down the bay. This trip, like all voyages of discovery, has been powerful, leaving us with many different, some new, some reassuring, some troubling images of this grand river and bay. As we cross delicate estuarine boundaries of fresh and salt water, where cod used to spawn, and where a few last lobsters are still trapped, a raw wind greets us from the southeast, and we have miles to go (and poets to meet) before we sleep at the head of the bay.

Boats for all seasons

The past year has been a period of significant improvements to our small but growing fleet. SANDERLING, a 19-foot aluminum Lund skiff, along with a new Yamaha 25-horsepower outboard and trailer, was donated by Mr. and Mrs. John Ames, and is a wonderfully versatile and cost-effective addition to our on-the-water capabilities. Primarily dedicated to the Science & Stewardship Program, SANDERLING can squeak into tight places where even FISH HAWK cannot venture, and being trailerable can be dispatched to distant locations with ease, safety and considerable savings of time and expense. Metal fabricators Steele & Marshall proved that engineering skill and ingenuity are still alive and well in our home port: their heavy grab bar makes for enhanced safety underway, and provides improved stowage and even a frame over which a tarp can be spread for overnighting aboard.

FISH HAWK saw reduced use this past year, primarily due to the acquisition of SANDERLING and increased use of RAVEN. Having been subjected to over seven years of demanding service with little in the way of improvements or service, this 26-foot workhorse is undergoing significant structural and minor cosmetic attention this spring and will see renewed use in the months and years ahead. The twin Yamaha 130's continue to turn in a sustained, flawless performance as does the Raytheon R20 radar. The remarkable quality of these units has added immeasurably to our peace of mind, safety and ability to "be there" in all but the worst conditions.

The majority of this year's improvement efforts went into RAVEN, which is now twice the boat she was at this time last year, thanks to the Norcross Wildlife Foundation Inc., whose restricted grant of $17,000 made possible the purchase of a new engine. Important systems additions or upgrades were made possible by the generosity of Institute trustee Betty Noyce, who not only donated the original funds for RAVEN's purchase but also created an account for maintenance and improvements. The mileage we've gotten from this account, now largely depleted, has been multiplied by the generosity of a number of individuals and institutions. Haywood May of Bass Harbor Marine has provided yard services at reduced rates, undertaken scavenging forays through his yard's sail loft and storage sheds, and made numerous successful solicitation calls on our behalf to chandleries and marine equipment manufacturers.

Chummy Rich's crew at adjacent Bass Harbor Boat, where all of the actual work was done, turned in a great performance; the design, engineering, workmanship and timing were consistently fine and made the entire endeavor a pleasure. Replacing RAVEN's old gasoline engine with a new Caterpillar 3116TA diesel has given us a 50 percent speed increase, and has decreased fuel consumption by 35 percent, halved maintenance costs, and eliminated the risk associated with onboard gasoline. Southworth-Milton of Scarborough provided the engine at a generous price. The Raytheon Corporation donated a new R20XX radar unit which is truly remarkable, especially when coupled with the Raychart 600 electronic chart unit made possible by Hamilton Marine of Searsport. Receiving satellite signals through our Magellan GPS, donated by Mr. and Mrs. David Donnan, allows us to "see" *exactly* where we are at all times; onboard demonstrations are yours for the asking when you see us. As RAVEN's skipper I must continually force myself to remember that these high-tech miracles are my back-up, not primary, navigation systems; along a coast like this nothing will ever take the place of a true compass, a watch, charts and common sense.

Other RAVEN improvements this year include expanded fuel capacity, a cellular phone provided by Unicel of Rockland, and — most wonderful of all — heat. The "character-building" and "mind-numbing" experience which has been referred to in previous *Journals* is largely a matter of the past, at least while the crew is aboard RAVEN, where no longer are we forced to sleep fully clothed inside two sleeping bags. Again, special thanks to Betty and Haywood. Deepest appreciation to all of those who have added to our ability to provide services along the coast; thanks to your faith in us and your thoughtful generosity, our on-the-water comfort, safety and reliability have improved by orders of magnitude.

— Peter Ralston

Over the years, our boat operations have been significantly enhanced by the occasional donation of vessels. These gifts have resulted either in boats we keep and use, or boats we convert into the funds necessary to run our existing fleet. Either way, we'd certainly like to hear from you if you should be in a position to consider such a gift.

Proprietors, Roosevelts, and Scoundrels

(continued from page 35)

Campobello islanders first heard about the "Arkansas travelers," as they became known locally, in the spring of 1984. Christopher Wade appeared at a chamber of commerce meeting that drew 200 people. There he outlined plans for a an initial 93-acre residential development, restaurants, marina, water slide, swimming and fishing lake, eventual construction of condos, hotel, medical center, recreational vehicle camping park and a 4,400-foot airstrip near Head Harbour. Eyebrows were raised especially high at the promise of a ski slope — on an island with no large hills and very little snow. Wade later described the ski slope as "the work of an overzealous brochure planner."

Not surprisingly, people were concerned. Approximately one-third of the island was slated for a scale and type of development unmatched along the Fundy coast and completely foreign to people's experience. People divided along "for" and "against" lines. Supporters saw the jobs potential in road-building (the road mileage was doubled by the Campobello Company) and house construction, as well as in the company office. Opponents were concerned about losing the island identity, not being able to afford to buy land, and not having anywhere to grow. And some were philosophical: "If this company hadn't bought the land, somebody else would have. All we are hoping is that the people who come here are easy to get along with."

Provincial politicians came on board early. Campobello's member of the New Brunswick Legislature at the time, mainlander Robert Jackson, was quoted in a newspaper as saying, "I see no reason to oppose American interests coming in. After all, American interests have owned parts of this island for years. . . . Even if they do half of what they say they will, it will be a major change in island life and some people will continue to oppose it because they can't accept change."

The provincial government went on to provide the company a $1,000-per-year lease on the extensive former summer estate of the Frederick Adams family, cousins of the Roosevelts, which it had acquired as part of the Herring Cove provincial park lands. Here the Campobello Company set up its headquarters and hosted potential buyers of island land. (This estate is now the Lupine Lodge, a charming summer lodging and dining establishment run by the

Stephen Muskie

The once bountiful groundfishery is virtually gone.

Lupine Corporation, a business controlled by local women.)

Campobello, like most of rural New Brunswick, does not have a local government. Instead it is designated a "local service district" under provincial regulation; it is essentially a protectorate of the Department of Municipalities, Culture and Housing. Since the province does not have specific land use regulations for unincorporated rural areas (except for water and sewage requirements), the only protection against undesirable activities is through local organizing and political pressure.

The idea of incorporating into a municipality that would have the power to zone land and regulate development had been raised on Campobello several times in the past, to no avail. Like rural people everywhere, islanders resist being restricted themselves in how they can use their own property. The belief that local governments mean more taxes is also widely held, since the municipality would be responsible for roads and other infrastructure.

The advantage of this live-and-let-live approach, as well as the slack provincial control over coastal land use on Campobello, was not lost on the Campobello Company. Company general manager Larry Kuca told the *Boston Globe*, "The developers acknowledge they chose Campobello partly because the island has no zoning or municipal government and because Canada's environmental and sewage requirements are not as strict as on islands off Maine's coast. . . . If this was an American island, I doubt we could be developing it. Here we have the cooperation of the government."

One incident suggests that the company was not above manipulating island politics to protect its interests. A petition was started in 1984 to ascertain the level of support for incorporating as a municipality. For a year the petition was mired inside the Department of Municipal Affairs. Finally a public meeting was scheduled for October, 1985, to discuss it. About a week before the meeting, islanders began receiving phone calls. On the other end of the line was an Arkansas university student conducting a survey of public opinion regarding the Campobello Company development. The final question asked was, If there were an election for mayor of Campobello, who would you vote for, Ralph Lord or Clifford Calder? Mr. Lord was a vocal opponent of the development and an advocate of incorporation; Mr. Calder was a vocal company supporter.

If there is anything rural people don't like it is a hidden agenda or in this case the appearance of one, especially among their own. While neither Mr. Lord nor Mr. Calder had given permission for their names to be used or expressed a desire to be mayor of Campobello, and while they jointly took out an ad in the local weekly newspaper to say so, the damage was done. The next week at the public meeting, they were both effectively muzzled. Suspicion was cast on the entire incorporation enterprise and, once again, it failed to get off the ground.

The Campobello Company denied any responsibility for this incident. The *St. Croix Courier* interviewed both Larry Kuca and James McDougal. According to Kuca, using Lord's and Calder's names in the survey "was totally unauthorized" and he said he put a stop to it as soon as he found out. He also said he called the two men to apologize. Ralph Lord says he never received such a call; Mr. Calder has since passed away. At the head office in Arkansas, McDougal said, "I was mortified . . . the last thing on earth we want to do is upset them. . . we don't think we're smarter than these people and we don't want to interfere in their affairs." McDougal claimed that although the company commissioned the survey to be done, he did not see the questions. In spite of the company's claims, the outcome of the public meeting on incorporation certainly served its interests: by its own admission, a local government would certainly have cramped its style.

Meanwhile, the third Campobello Company's grandiose scheme got scaled back dramatically, to primarily land subdivision and sale of house lots. By 1986, Kuca was describing the project as "a non-commercial, natural-type development targeting the 'summer retreat' market." Perhaps investors were harder to find than anticipated. In any case, local concerns continued to plague company management. Larry Kuca's frustration was thinly veiled in an Augusta, Maine, *Kennebec Journal* article of October, 1985, when he said, "We are a sensitive developer and we want to work with the community but you can't please everybody in this kind of situation. I know one thing — you can't sell lots easily if everybody on the island is running around bad-mouthing you, so we have to be concerned."

For two years this latest incarnation of the Campobello Company moved forward. Roads were built and utility lines put in. At the peak of activity, 60 people were employed in land clearing, road-building and on phone duty at the sales office. Land was surveyed into various sized lots, from one acre to up to 15. Ten- to 15-acre oceanfront, clifftop tracts were advertised for $50,000; one- and three acre lots were available from $6,000 to $15,000 depending on location. Financing was provided with as little as 1 percent down at a fixed rate of 9.5 percent for 15 years through the Madison Guarantee Savings and Loan. Television ads ran in Arkansas and New England. "An island paradise awaits you on Campobello Island, Franklin Delano Roosevelt's 'beloved island,'" the sales brochure advised prospective customers. "You can now own a piece of the history that inspired the dreams of a President." Many initial buyers from Arkansas bought sight unseen.

Late in 1986 the boom fell. U.S. federal regulators, suspicious of the real estate liabilities of the Madison Savings and Loan, seized its assets including the Campobello Company land holdings. While exact figures are hard to pin down, approximately 222 house lots had been surveyed by that

Campobello islanders first heard about the "Arkansas travelers," as they became known locally, in the spring of 1984.

time. Although some 70 of the lots had been sold, only a few houses had been built. The remaining Campobello Company land went into bureaucratic limbo.

Federal documents show that it was Campobello that pushed Madison Guarantee Savings and Loan over the edge, not the much smaller but more notorious 230-acre Whitewater development. Federal payouts to Madison customers when it failed totaled $60 million. In 1989, the U.S. government set up the Resolution Trust Corporation (RTC) to handle the real estate that came into federal hands when savings and loans across the country failed. Of the Campobello Company's original purchase of 3,900 acres, 3,419 acres landed in the lap of the RTC. Its book value (probably inflated, according to an RTC official) was listed as $2.7 million in 1987. Appeals to the U.S. government for special consideration of island interests went nowhere, in spite of some favorable early signs. Because of the nature of the land, it became subject to conditions under the Coastal Barriers Improvement Act. According to law, the property was first listed in the Federal Register.

For 90 days, only U.S. government agencies and non-profit conservation organizations were able to submit notices of interest to purchase. Canadian conservation non-profits that are registered as charities in the United States (of which there are few) were also eligible for the restricted first refusal. Following that time, a 90-day negotiation period would have been provided had any notices of interest been received. If a purchase price had been negotiated, no Canadian buyers would have had a chance to bid at all.

In New Brunswick, the exclusion of potential Canadian purchasers from the first refusal process did not play well. A headline in the provincial daily, the

Telegraph Journal, read, "Locals need not apply: Canadians are shut out of Campobello land sale." Curtis Newman of the Campobello chamber of commerce reiterated islanders' concern that a private American interest could once again monopolize the land to the exclusion of islanders. Linda Godfrey, a long-time American landowner on Campobello and volunteer with the Campobello Heritage Committee, was quoted as saying, "This is the last opportunity the islanders have to control their own destiny. I think that in the spirit of Franklin and Eleanor Roosevelt [the U.S.] has an obligation to them."

In January, a *Telegraph Journal* headline announced what was probably inevitable: "American purchases one-third of Campobello." The buyer, Mike Kaiser, was a Californian who had retired eight years earlier to Deer Isle, Maine, and had recently built a house on Casco Bay Island off Campobello's western shore. "I'm not a developer," he told the *St. Croix Courier*. "I didn't envision buying this much property and now that I have, I view it as an investment and don't want to be destructive in any way." He didn't want to be "the king of Campobello," he told the paper, explaining that his original intent had been to buy 300 to 400 acres on Campobello, but that the RTC had insisted on selling all of the third Campobello Company's holdings as a package. Kaiser paid $1.1 million for the land. Tentatively, the *Courier* reported, he planned to put about 100 of the previously subdivided lots on the market in the spring of 1995.

EPILOGUE

Campobello is now at a crossroads. Factors within and beyond island control will influence which road islanders take. The past could repeat itself if the new owner proves to be insensitive; benevolence on his part might produce a reasonable arrangement with local interests. Meanwhile, movements afoot in the provincial government could place restrictions on what can be done with the land this time around. A coastal zone management policy is being developed and rural communities may be forced to organize under new "rural municipality" structures in the near future, so that land use plans can be developed and enforced.

Meanwhile, islanders could assert some control by incorporating as a municipality now, without waiting for the provincial regulations to come into force. Short of owning the land outright, establishing some local control over the future of the island is perhaps the only route open to them.

Janice Harvey is a freelance writer in St. Stephen, New Brunswick.

REVIEWS

How one Maine landscape gave itself to the world of art

The Artist's Mount Desert: American Painters on the Maine Coast, by John Wilmerding. Princeton, New Jersey: Princeton University Press, 1994. 195 pages.

Reviewed by Pamela J. Belanger

John Wilmerding's long-awaited study makes available to a national audience what Mainers have long known — that Mount Desert is a special American landscape. Like Niagara Falls, the Yosemite Valley, Yellowstone or other geographically unique places, this wilderness island inspired several generations of American artists from the Hudson River School, through the Impressionists and early 20th century modernists, to contemporary artists.

His wide-ranging survey of artists' views and representations of the first national park on the eastern seaboard provides an overview of changing styles of art, and helps us to understand better why Mount Desert has become the scenic tourist Mecca it is today.

A member of the art history faculty at Princeton, John Wilmerding is well suited to uncover this national art treasure. His affection for Mount Desert is evident (he has a house there), and his book presents a sweeping appreciation for the place he knows and loves, and for the artists and styles he has devoted his career to studying.

Beginning with the early history of Mount Desert, Wilmerding discusses the island's natural history, its early explorers and settlement, and the innovations in transportation that increased the public's — and artists' — accessibility to this remote spot. The careers and work of early explorer-artists such as Thomas Birch, Thomas Doughty, and Alvan Fisher in the early decades of the nineteenth century are well documented.

A second wave of artists had taken the island wilderness as their subject by the middle of the 19th century. Thomas Cole, Fitz Hugh Lane, Frederick Edwin Church and William Stanley Haseltine made pioneering contributions to American art while making the island better known, and it is in these chapters that his mastery of his subject is most vividly apparent.

In the latter part of the 19th century, a veritable flood of artists followed the footsteps of these early discoverers, and Wilmerding's study includes both well-known and lesser-known painters. A diverse and fascinating group, they included such greats and near-greats as John Henry Hill, Aaron Draper Shattuck, William M. Hart, Sanford R. Gifford, William Trost Richards, Samuel Lancaster Gerry, Andrew Warren, W.W. Brown, David Maitland Armstrong, F.O.C. Darley, Henry Waugh, Alfred Thompson Bricher, Xanthus Smith, George H. Smillie, Ralph Blakelock, Louis Comfort Tiffany, John La Farge, and Childe Hassam. The book's many illustrations of their work provide a rich and delightful perspective on the changing styles of American art from Luminism to Impressionism.

In his concluding chapter, Wilmerding turns to the radical changes in style that characterize the work of a special group of modernists who brought their innovative perspectives in art to the representation of Mount Desert. He highlights the work of Allen Tucker, Carroll Tyson, William Zorach, Oscar Bluemner, John Marin, Marsden Hartley, and the contemporary artist Richard Estes.

The Artist's Mount Desert will be an essential addition to any library with a focus on the Maine and New England Coast, and it will be especially useful to art historians, curators and collectors seeking to better understand how painters found pictorial means for representing what Thomas Cole called in 1845 "the grandest coast scenery we have found."

Pamela J. Belanger is a member of the staff at the Farnsworth Art Museum in Rockland.

Getting there and back, with care and respect

The Cruising Guide to the New England Coast, Eleventh Edition, by Roger F. Duncan, Paul W. Fenn, W. Wallace Fenn and John P. Ware. New York: W. W. Norton, 1995.

Reviewed by David D. Platt

Coastal guidebooks seem to have established themselves as a literary genre in this region as early as the 17th century, when explorers like Weymouth, Rosier and John Smith described what they had seen for their patrons and others back home. Their books were intended largely for armchair mariners; the authors of more modern guides aim their words at people who intend to do their own exploring.

The change in audiences is significant. Writers of guidebooks, particularly books that cover fragile places like Maine islands, bear a heavy responsibility these days, because a mere mention in a cruising guide, particularly an overly enthusiastic one, can bring the hordes to spots that can't sustain them.

Having been involved with the *Cruising Guide to the New England Coast* for much of his adult life (his father was one

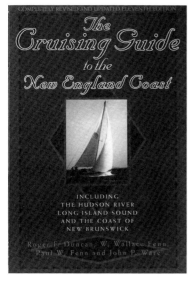

of its original authors), Roger Duncan understands the guidebook writer's burden better than most. I have been reading and using various editions of the *Cruising Guide* for 25 years or so, and can report that his latest effort — the 11th edition — is, in terms of its sensitivity to island residents' needs at least, the best yet.

Environmental concern permeates the book. From the dedication ("to all those who, cruising the coast, love it and seek to preserve it") to the final pages, the authors urge respect for coastal residents' privacy, for the needs of wildlife, for the rights of those who depend on the waters the reader might visit.

"Fundamental changes are taking place on the New England coast and the rate of change is accelerating," the authors write. "The islands, capes and ledges still lie where they were moored centuries ago, but the harbors and the shores around them are not the same." They list some of the changes: more boats, manned by less experienced skippers; fewer uncrowded anchorages; automated lighthouses; coastal development and the shift to a tourist economy; fewer places to take on fuel and water; fewer small grocery stores; the dramatic decline of parts of the fishing industry and the resulting growth of regulations. "And in many towns," they note for the benefit of the skipper who hasn't visited lately, "you now need a license to go clamming."

Not all the changes have been negative, as Duncan and Co. are quick to point out. Aquaculture has come into its own along the Maine and New Brunswick coasts in the past decade, and despite the risks associated with it, the authors regard it as an important new element in the region's economy.

Two additions since the 10th edition are noteworthy: numerous photographs, including aerials that should help sailors find their way in and out of tight spots; and an excellent chapter on wildlife by Bill Hancock of the Maine Audubon Society. (Earlier editions included a similar chapter entitled "Birding Under Sail" by another Maine Audubon staffer, but Hancock's version is far more comprehensive.)

The Cruising Guide to the New England Coast covers a lot of territory and can't hope to be as detailed as a guide limited to Maine. Still, it contains a staggering amount of information including detailed sailing directions for "inside" and "outside" passages along the coast as well as "local knowledge" about entering tiny harbors with unmarked hazards.

Since its earliest editions in the 1930s the *Cruising Guide* has stressed history, local lore and even legend nearly as much as the how-to-get-there stuff. Despite the changes and the more up-to-date look of this edition,

longtime admirers of this book's anecdotal style needn't worry: the weather-wise fishermen, Harvard presidents and ghosts are all still here. It may have been written for the skipper in need of a guide for his trip to the Maine coast, but in fact, *The Cruising Guide to the New England Coast* is just as good an armchair read as anything by Capt. John Smith.

Lighthouses: working-class heroes

Lighthouse . . . Ten Wood Engravings by Siri Beckman. Stonington, Maine: Out of the Woods Press, 1993.

Reviewed by John Ames

Sometimes I feel sorry for lighthouses. These no-nonsense protectors from the dark and dirty weather of earlier days now often find themselves reduced to bluebird day clichés by legions of well-meaning but ocean-ignorant summer painters. No other coastal icon suffers such artistic ignominy with the possible exception of the lobster boat.

Maine lighthouses are, or at least were, in the business of generating huge shafts of light for the purpose of preventing property damage and loss of human life. They did very serious work. Seri Beckman knows the reasons for lighthouses and portrays them as real working-class heroes in her wonderful, tiny, artist book, *Lighthouse . . .Ten Wood Engravings*.

Beckman was inspired to do her inch-and-five-eighths square engravings by Gary Hamel, whose remembrances of Curtis Island Light prompted her to think of a lighthouse as a "metaphor of light and dark, safety and danger." The artist starts with dense, brooding images of 10 well-known lights including Nubble, Portland Head and Marshall Point. The time of day in each portrait is night and the sky is angry. Then in each work she carves out one letter of the word "lighthouse." What makes these little prints so striking is that the scale of each stark, white letter is very large compared to the overall image, giving the impression of a very bright beam of light stabbing the overall gloom. It is very effective printmaking.

The edition is cut from maple and boxwood blocks and is printed in an edition of 100.

For further information about this book contact Out of the Woods Press, P.O. Box 335, Stonington, Maine 04861

November Sun

PHILIP BOOTH

A raw dawn. Hard wind
poured out of the North,
bright whitecaps riding
the Bay all morning,
a new coldfront wedging
through:
    roll after roll
of stratocumulus, come over
a thousand miles of
Canada, unfurling
across the Bay.
Out of the clouds'
flat undersides, over
Belfast and back of
Megunticook, quick
slants of mussel-blue
rain. Slant after slant,
they all evaporate
on the way
down.
    To the Sou'west,
East of Deer Isle, South
of Devil's Head, across
the channel called
Eggemoggin, out into
Jerico Bay, fallen
sunlight keeps falling:
as far as a human eye
can try not to go blind,
the sky is blue beyond
blue, the sea become
hammered gold. Gold
unto gold until,
beyond Whaleback Ledge,
West Halibut Rock and
Saddleback, beyond
the horizon's barely
discernible curve,
there's all the rest,
the spun rest, of
the world.

    Back here
on Dump Hill, back
in the Town Dump's
Dump Shack, Captain
Durward, now retired
to recycling, Cooler's
boy, and Norwood Caine
and the Mayor of
Hardscrabble, here in
his trademark derby,
snug-up close to the
pot-stove, bemoaning
Perot-votes lost between
here and Texas, calling
by their illegitimate
names every Spotted
Owl freak between
Oregon's Portland
and Maine's.
    Here, parked
next to the shack, in
the back of an old blue
pickup without any
tailgate, a black part-lab
half rolled on her side,
lies in the lee of the
cab, soaking up sun,
November sun. For now,
maybe feeling summer
long gone, she lolls
her head up on the
wheel-well as if she
were Bangor's prime
animal Rescue League
model: living life
as it's given,
    letting
pure being become her.

From Pairs *by Philip Booth, published by Viking Penguin Books, 1995.*
Reprinted with permission.

ISLAND INSTITUTE • 60 Ocean St., Rockland, ME 04841 • (207)594-9209
MEMBERSHIP

___$40 MEMBER	___$100 CONTRIBUTOR	___$1,000 SUSTAINER
___$40 NON-PROFIT ORGANIZATION	___$250 DONOR	___$2,500 BENEFACTOR
___$60 SUBSCRIBER	___$500 GUARANTOR	___$5,000 PATRON

Canadian residents please add $10 for shipping, all other countries add $15 U.S.

Name_____

Phone _____

Permanent address _____

City, State, Zip _____

Summer mailing address* _____

City, State, Zip _____

Do you own island property? Yes ____ No ____ Island name _____

Method of payment: Check ____ Visa/MC # _____ exp._____

Signature _____

*Benefits will be mailed to this address from June 1 through September 1.
Island Institute is a recognized non-profit organization, however, under current IRS regulations, all but $32.95 will be tax deductible,
reflecting the actual value of the membership benefits you will receive (see reverse).

ISLAND INSTITUTE • 60 Ocean St., Rockland, ME 04841 • (207)594-9209
GIFT MEMBERSHIP

___$40 MEMBER	___$100 CONTRIBUTOR	___$1,000 SUSTAINER
___$40 NON-PROFIT ORGANIZATION	___$250 DONOR	___$2,500 BENEFACTOR
___$60 SUBSCRIBER	___$500 GUARANTOR	___$5,000 PATRON

Canadian residents please add $10 for shipping, all other countries add $15 U.S.

Recipient's name _____

Permanent address _____

City, State, Zip _____

Summer mailing address* _____

City, State, Zip _____

Your name _____ Phone _____

Permanent address _____

City, State, Zip _____

Method of payment: Check ____ Visa/MC # _____ exp._____

Signature _____

*Benefits will be mailed to this address from June 1 through September 1.
Island Institute is a recognized non-profit organization, however, under current IRS regulations, all but $32.95 will be tax deductible,
reflecting the actual value of the membership benefits you will receive (see reverse).

Available in July, 1995:

FROM CAPE COD TO THE BAY OF FUNDY

AN ENVIRONMENTAL ATLAS OF THE GULF OF MAINE

Edited by Philip W. Conkling • Published by MIT Press and Island Institute

See reverse for ordering information

ISLAND INSTITUTE   MEMBERSHIP BENEFITS

- **ISLAND JOURNAL** — Our nationally acclaimed, award-winning annual publication, featuring photographs, essays, stories, poetry, and interviews with island people.

- **INTER-ISLAND NEWS** — A bi-monthly publication filled with timely issues and information for and about the islands and their communities

- **THE WORKING WATERFRONT** — A bi-monthly newspaper aimed at informing members and coastal residents about marine resource topics which directly affect coastal economies.

- **CONFERENCES, LECTURES** — Invitations will be sent to our annual conference, winter lecture series, and other educational programs given throughout the year.

- Color decal for your car.

For contributions of $100, 10% of your donation will go directly toward funding of Island Institute's Island Schools Scholarship Fund.

ISLAND INSTITUTE   MEMBERSHIP BENEFITS

- **ISLAND JOURNAL** — Our nationally acclaimed, award-winning annual publication, featuring photographs, essays, stories, poetry, and interviews with island people.

- **INTER-ISLAND NEWS** — A bi-monthly publication filled with timely issues and information for and about the islands and their communities

- **THE WORKING WATERFRONT** — A bi-monthly newspaper aimed at informing members and coastal residents about marine resource topics which directly affect coastal economies.

- **CONFERENCES, LECTURES** — Invitations will be sent to our annual conference, winter lecture series, and other educational programs given throughout the year.

- Color decal for your car.

For contributions of $100, 10% of your donation will go directly toward funding of Island Institute's Island Schools Scholarship Fund.

FROM CAPE COD TO THE BAY OF FUNDY
AN ENVIRONMENTAL ATLAS OF THE GULF OF MAINE

Edited by Philip W. Conkling • Published by MIT Press and Island Institute

With beautiful images and accessible text, this book surveys the ecology of the land
and waters of the New England and Southeastern Canadian coasts.
272 pages, 173 illustrations (135 color, 38 black & white).

Available July 1995 ⑤ Order yours today!

Send me ___ copies of the Environmental Atlas!

❑ Paperback $29.95   ❑ Cloth cover $50.00

Please add $3.50 shipping. Maine residents add 6% sales tax.

Name _____

Address _____

City, State, Zip _____

Method of payment ❑ Check ❑ Visa/MC # _____ exp._____

ISLAND INSTITUTE • 60 Ocean Street, Rockland ME 04841 • (207) 594-9209